THE
CODE

ABOUT THE AUTHOR:

JASON ROGERS GREW UP IN A SMALL TOWN, DUE WEST OF CHICAGO. HE'S A HUSBAND, FATHER, AVID MARTIAL ARTIST, ADVENTURE SEEKER, CIGAR SMOKER, EXTREME SPORTS GUY, & ENTREPRENEUER, WHO GREW UP LABELED AS "WITHOUT A FUTURE". BEING A HIGH SCHOOL DROP OUT, FREINDS OF SMUGGLERS, BIKERS, MOB GUYS, AND ALL KINDS OF COLORFUL CHARACTERS IN BETWEEN LEFT HIM QUESTIONING LIFE AND WHAT'S OUT THERE. IT WAS THIS VERY THIRST FOR NOT ACCEPTING THE STATUS QUO WHICH CAUSED HIM TO PURSUE AND CHALLANGE EVERYTHING THAT SEEMED DESIGNED TO "WALL HIM IN".

JASON IS CURRENTLY RETIRED, LIVING IN EUROPE, SPENDING THE MAJORITY OF HIS TIME WITH HIS WIFE AND RAISING HIS CHILDEREN AND OBVIOUSLY WRITING BOOKS.

CONTENTS

INTRODUCTION

BADEN WÜRTTEMBERG: 05:59 31:10:2018

PULLING NO PUNCHES, THIS BOOK MOST CERTAINLY APPLIES TO EVERYONE.

I DECIDED TO WRITE THIS BOOK BECAUSE I FELT SOMEONE NEEDED TO LET MEN KNOW THAT IT'S OK TO BE MEN. KICK THE PENDULUM THE OTHER WAY FOR A CHANGE, AND NOT SIMPLY JUST FOR MEN AS THE PRINCIPLES PERTAIN TO LITERALLY EVERYONE IN EVERY WALK OF LIFE...

THIS BOOK IS SIMPLY A BOOK OF TRUTH'S. IF EMBRACED, IT WILL REVOLUTIONIZE YOUR LIFE... IT DID MINE.

THE OLD ADAGE, YOU CAN GIVE MAN A FISH AND FEED HIM FOR A DAY...TEACH A MAN TO FISH AND YOU'LL FEED HIM FOR A LIFETIME...

I COULD WRITE A BOOK BUILDING YOU UP ALL DAY... MAKE YOU FEEL GREAT!... BUT IT'S BETTER TO SHOW YOU HOW TO MEND AND RE- BREAK (IF NEEDED) YOUR OWN FRACTURES, SEW YOUR OWN SUTURE'S, AND SHOW YOU HOW TO FIGHT SO THAT YOU CAN SELF ARREST, RE-WIRE SOME STUFF AND GET FIXED... I HOPE THIS BOOK BUILDS UP AND STRENGTHENS EVERYONE ELSE AS NEEDED...YOU HAVE TO BREAK DOWN A MUSCLE IN ORDER TO BUILD IT...

AND FOR SOME PEOPLE... SOMETIMES YOU NEED TO GO BACK IN ORDER TO GO FORWARD... YOU NEED TO PICK UP SOME THINGS YOU LEFT ALONG THE WAY...

THE HYBRID OF THE KEYS IN THIS BOOK ARE WHAT MAKES FOR AN EXCITING LIFE. QUALIFY THE THINGS YOU READ IN THIS BOOK. IF IT RESONATES, TAKE THE PRINCIPLES, & PROCESSES, MAKING THEM YOURS. DON'T SIMPLY JUST READ AND DO IT... YOU'LL COME UP SHORT. TRUE CHANGE MEANS OWNERSHIP. RUN WITH YOUR OWN FOUNDATION BECAUSE, THEN AT THAT POINT YOU ARE STABLE AND CAN ACHIEVE THE THINGS IN YOUR HEART. WHY? BECAUSE YOU OWN IT.

WHAT MAKES A MAN A MAN? OPINIONS VERY... I WOULDN'T DEFINE A MAN BY SUCCESS IN IT'S

PUREST FORM OR IDEOLOGY. I WOULD HOWEVER DEFINE HIM BY HIM LIVING A LIFE OF PERSONAL INTEGRITY, & RELENTLESS DEDICATION. MEANING, HE STICKS TO HIS PRINCIPLES EVEN UNTIL DEATH. MY GUESS, BY NATURE, IN LARGE PART DUE TO TESTOSTERONE...MEN ARE FIGHTERS, CONQUEROR'S, & INHERINTLY TERRITORIAL. THE PERSONAL PRIDE (INWARD VALUES) WE HAVE ARE OUR OWN PERSONAL MEASURING STICK. LIVING BY THESE VALUES IS A CONSTANT FIGHT. ACHIEVING, OR MAINTAINING THEM IS THE FUEL BY WHICH WE STAND AND HOLD OUR HEAD HIGH. OUR STANDARD. OUR SEAL OF APPROVAL.... THE TRUE HEART OF PATRIOTISM. IT'S ALL ABOUT OUR BANNER OR COLORS...THE FLAG WE FLY

COMFORT KILLS

DON'T EVER LET YOURSELF BE COMFORTABLE.
I BELIEVE IT'S ALWAYS GOOD TO TEST YOURSELF
EVERYDAY. DO SOMETHING SIMPLY BECUASE
YOU DON'T WANT TO. SOMETHING OUT OF
YOUR COMFORT ZONE. MAKE IT A RULE. IT CAN
BE OPENING A DOOR FOR SOMEONE, DOING
SOMETHING TODAY AS OPPOSED TO TOMORROW,
READING FOR 5 MIN SOMETHING YOU'D RATHER
NOT MAKING SURE YOU GET SOMETHING OUT OF
IT, OR WHILE ON YOUR WAY TO BED AT 0300 GET
UP AND GO OUTSIDE AND GO FOR A RUN SIMPLY
BECAUSE IT'S RANDOM, UNCOMFORTABLE AND
THE LAST THING IN THE WORLD YOU'D RATHER DO
RIGHT NOW. IF YOU DECIDE TO OPEN A DOOR FOR
SOMEONE WHEN YOU'D RATHER NOT, WHETHER
IT BE BECUASE YOU HATE THAT PERSON OR
SIMPLY JUST DON'T WANT TO OPEN A DOOR FOR

SOMEONE, DO IT. DON'T DO IT FOR THEM. DON'T DO IT FOR ANY ACCOLADES OR RESPONSE. DO IT SIMPLY BECUASE IT'S YOUR RULE. WHETHER YOU SMILE EXTERNALLY, INTERNALLY, OR NOT AT ALL (LOL) WHILE ACCOMPLISHING THIS RULE. DO SO KNOWING THAT IT'S BECUASE, YOU ACCOMPLISHED YOUR RULE AND YOU HAVE HONORED YOURSELF BY DOING SO (STAYING TRU).

BEING COMFORTABLE TOO LONG ALLOWS YOU TO BE COMPLACENT. THE HUMAN BODY IS SO MUCH MORE RESILIENT THAN WE THINK. THE HUMAN BODY CAN TAKE SO MUCH MORE THAN WE GIVE IT CREDIT FOR. IT'S JUST THAT NO ONE PUSHES THE LIMITS TO SEE WHAT THEIR'S CAN ACTUALLY DO. JUST LIKE IN TRAINING, NEVER LET YOURSELF PLATEAU. YOU WANT TO FOREVER BE IN A STATE OF ALWAYS PUSHING. TIL THE DAY YOU DIE. IF YOU DON'T USE IT, YOU LOSE IT AS THEY SAY. MOST INJURIES HAPPEN BECAUSE YOU TOOK TOO LONG A BREAK. MOST PEOPLE HEAR AN AGE AND THEN QUIT WHEN THEY FINALLY GET THERE IF NOT BEFORE. BECUASE, THEY THINK THEY'RE TOO OLD AND THAT NUMBER SETS THE LIMIT. YOU HAVE TO KEEP PUSHING. YEAR'S AGO, WHEN I WAS A MAILMAN, I KILLED IT. I USUALLY RAN(LITERALLY) 2 ROUTES A DAY OR ONE HUGE ROUTE THAT

MOST COULDN'T DO BY THEMSELVES, FOLLOWED BY HELPING ON OTHER ROUTES AFTER. I THINK I WAS 33 THEN... I WORKED WITH THIS GUY. HE WAS 67. HE COULD EASILY HANG WITH ME. EASILY. IT'S BECAUSE HE ALWAYS STAYED BUSY. HE GREW UP STARTING A CONSTRUCTION COMPANY, THEN HE BECAME A PILOT FOR SOME INDIAN PRINCE FLYING ALL ACROSS THE PLANET. HE HAD RECENTLY GOTTEN GROUNDED BY THE F.A.A. FOR CONTRACTING SOME INFECTION IN HIS HEART FROM SOME BUG IN THE JUNGLE. IN THE INTERIM OF HIM GETTING HIS FLIGHT CLEARANCE AGAIN, HE TOOK UP THE MAILMAN GIG. I COMMENTED TO HIM ONE DAY, "DUDE, YOU KILL THIS...NO OFFENSE BUT FOR YOUR AGE..." HE THEN TOLD ME IT'S BECAUSE HE ALWAYS STAYED BUSY. EVEN AS A PILOT HE WOULD WALK, LIFT, & HIKE, EVERYDAY.

THE HUMAN BODY IS CAPABLE OF SO MUCH MORE THAN WE GIVE IT CREDIT FOR. IT CAN WITHSTAND A LOT. A...LOT... THE BIGGEST ENEMY IS US AND THE LIMITS WE ALLOW TO BE PUT ON OURSELVES WHETHER BY OTHERS AND/OR OURSELVES INDIVIDUALLY. IN A MOVIE I'D WATCHED YEARS AGO, (GREAT MOVIE TOO). "ONCE YOU'VE TAKEN A FEW PUNCHES AND REALIZE YOUR NOT MADE OF GLASS, YOU DON'T

FEEL ALIVE UNLESS YOU'RE PUSHING YOURSELF AS FAR AS YOU CAN GO"-GREEN STREET HOOLIGANS. STUFF'S GOING TO HAPPEN. BUT ONCE YOU MAKE UP YOUR MIND TO NOT REACT. YOU'LL REALIZE THAT IT WASN'T THAT BAD, AND THE NEXT OBSTICALS WON'T SEEM AS HARD (YOU'LL GRADUATE).

THE CODE

EVERY MAN NEEDS A CODE. A STANDARD, SELF-PARAMETERS,OPERATING PROCEDURES, PROTOCOLS, RULES, KATA.

YOU HAVE TO BE TRU TO YOURSELF FIRST OR YOU'LL NEVER BE TRU TO ANYONE.

IF YOU DON'T BE TRU TO YOURSELF, YOU'LL NEVER BE TRU TO ANYONE OR ANYTHING CAUSING YOU TO FLOUNDER IN LIFE OR AT THE VERY LEAST NEVER WALK IN YOUR POTENTIAL. IF YOUR NOT TRU TO YOURSELF, YOU CAN NEVER REALLY BE TRUSTED. IF YOU NEVER BE TRU TO YOURSELF, YOU'LL NEVER KNOW WHO YOU REALLY ARE. NOR WILL ANYONE ELSE.

A PERSON'S IDENTITY IS DEFINED BY HIS PARAMETERS AND HOW HE KEEPS THEM. THE NATURAL OUTCOME OF WHAT YOU CHOOSE TO DO OR NOT DO WILL BE A HONEING AND

ISOLATION OF YOUR LIFE AND THUS IT'S COURSE. PARAMETERS CAN BE CHANGED.

ONE OF THE BIGGEST PROBLEMS TODAY IN SOCIETY IS THAT NO ONE KNOWS WHO THEY REALLY ARE. BEFORE YOUR ABLE TO DETERMINE WHAT IT IS YOU NEED TO CHANGE IF ANYTHING AT ALL, YOU HAVE TO KNOW WHAT YOU'RE WORKING WITH, KNOW WHAT YOU REALLY CURRENTLY ARE... THE EASIEST WAY TO DO THAT IS TO KNOW FIRST WHAT YOU AREN'T. WHAT IS IT WHERIN YOU DRAW THE LINE MORALLY? THAT'S NOT YOU, MOVE ON... WHAT IS IT THAT YOU KNOW YOU SIMPLY DON'T HAVE A SKILL FOR? AND I'M NOT SAYING SOMETHING YOU DON'T HAVE A SKILL FOR BECAUSE SOMEONE TOLD YOU THAT ONE DAY AND SO YOU'VE NEVER GIVEN IT A FAIR SHAKE... THAT'S ALSO WHAT YOUR NOT.

EVERYONE ALWAYS OBSESSES WITH WHAT YOUR NOT, IE. THE THINGS YOU'VE DONE WRONG & MISTAKES MADE, THE THINGS THAT DON'T MEET THE STANDARD OF WHAT EVERYONE ELSE THINKS YOU SHOULD BE BUT, YOU AREN'T. YOU ALREADY KNOW WHAT THOSE THINGS ARE AS YOU'VE HEARD, BEEN COMPARED TO, OR HAD THEM THROWN IN YOUR FACE FOR YEARS IF NOT YOUR ENTIRE LIFE. THERE'S ROOM/TIME TO

CHANGE ALL THAT LATER IF NEED BE. HOWEVER, SOME THINGS JUST WON'T FIT. I'VE OFTEN SEEN PEOPLE WASTE THEIR ENTIRE LIFE HOARDING VIRTUE THAT DOESN'T BELONG TO THEM. TRYING TO FIT A SQUARE PEG IN A ROUND HOLE.

ALMOST LIKE A PLAGUE, SO MANY ARE SO AFRAID TO BE THEMSELVES THAT THEY TRY TO BECOME EVERYONE ELSE...

SO. MANY. PEAPLE. WASTE INSURMOUNTABLE TIME & ENERGY, GREIVING, STRESSING, BEATING THEMSELVES UP OVER THINGS THAT THEY HAVE NO BUSINESS DOING, NOR TRYING TO ATTAIN. SOME THINGS ARE SIMPLY NOT IN THE CARDS FOR SOME PEAPLE. THAT'S NOT A PROBLEM BECAUSE, WE ALL HAVE A HAND TO PLAY. BEFORE YOU CAN DISCARD AND ADD TOO THAT HAND, YOU NEED TO DETERMINE WHAT YOUR HOLE CARDS ARE. (THE THINGS YOU KNOW YOU ARE AND THAT WORK FOR YOU). HOW YOU DO THAT IS "ALWAY'S BE YOURSELF, EXPRESS YOURSELF, HAVE FAITH IN YOURSELF. DO NOT GO OUT AND LOOK FOR A SUCCESSFUL PERSONALITY AND DUPLICATE IT". -BRUCE LEE IF ANYONE HAS EVER WATCHED THE SWORD AND THE STONE OR KING ARTHUR THE SWORD REPRESENTS IDENTITY. IT'S MISSING ITS OWNER.

THE STONE REPRESENTS THE WORLD AND EVERYTHING SET UP TESTING THE METAL OF OUR OWN PERSONAL VALUES. SOME PEOPLE NEVER LOOK FOR THE BOOK. SOME PEOPLE NEVER OPEN THE BOOK. SOME PEOPLE NEVER FIND THE SWORD. SOME PEOPLE NEVER PASS THE TEST AND FIND THAT MAGIC PLACE WHEN IT IS THAT WE FINALLY DECIDE TO OWN WHO WE ARE. HONED BY THE HARD PLACES AND STORMS OF THIS LIFE, SOMETHING BEAUTIFUL HAPPENS... THE GLEAMING RADIANCE OF AUTHORITY EMERGES WHEN, IN THE FACE OF EVERYTHING THE WARRIOR REMAINS TRU TO HIMSELF AND HIS PERSONAL VALUES. HIS CODE.

IDENTITY IS AUTHORITY.

WITHOLDING WHAT YOU ADD TO PEOPLE'S LIVES IS ACTUALLY 100% SELFISH. NEVER BE AFRAID TO JUST BE YOU. EVERYONE PLAYS A PART. EVERYONE HAS A PIECE IN THE PUZZLE & THE PUZZLE IS ALWAYS AT A DEFICIT WHEN ONE PIECE IS OFF OR MISSING...

PART OF THE WORLD'S FASCINATION WITH MOB MOVIES IS THAT THERE'S AN INWARD DESIRE IN EVERY MAN TO BE A MAN OF HONOR OR (CARRY HIMSELF WITH HONOR AND SELF- RESPECT HOLDING HIS HEAD HIGH, BACK STRAIGHT,

SHOULDERS SQUARE. A STAND-UP GUY. IF NOT, THEN FIGURING OUT WHY IS DEFINITLY WHERE YOU SHOULD START. BEING ABLE TO CARRY YOURSELF WITH PRIDE IS SOMETHING THAT YOUR FATHER, FRIENDS, FAMILY, CITY, JOB, RACE, HERITAGE, ASSOCIATIONS, ORGANIZATIONS, RELIGIONS ETC. ETC. CAN ALL GIVE YOU TO SOME DEGREE. HOWEVER, YOU'RE ACTUALLY DOING EVERYONE OR ANYONE OF THESE THINGS A DISSERVICE IF THE THINGS THAT MAKE THEM UP ARE NOT HARD WIRED INTO YOUR CORE. IN ORDER TO BE DOWN FOR ANYONE OR ANYTHING YOU FIRST HAVE TO TAKE OWNERSHIP IN YOURSELF AND BE COMFORTABLE IN YOUR OWN SKIN. ANYTHING LESS THAN THAT IS A PERSON WALKING IN DEFEAT, SELF-DENIAL AND A FRAUD. "EVERY MAN IS BORN AN ORIGINAL, SADLY MOST MEN DIE AS COPIES" -ABE LINCOLN. EVERYONE IS CREATED UNIQUE/ ORIGINAL IN THE SAME MANNER ALL DNA IS UNIQUE/ORIGINAL. A PERSON CAN NEVER LET THEMSELVES BE DEFINED BY THEIR HISTORY.

EVERYONE CAN BE A BAD ASS. FORGET WHAT YOU KNOW. PRESS FORWARD INTO WHO YOU ARE. SKY'S THE LIMIT.

I GREW UP IN A SMALL TOWN JUST WEST OF CHICAGO. IF I DIDN'T WEAR CONCERT T-SHIRTS,

HOLY JEANS, HAVE LONG HAIR, LISTEN TO HEAVY METAL MUSIC AND SMOKE CIGARETT'S AT 10 I'D GET BEAT UP. NO QUESTION.

ALL THAT BEING SAID. YOUR NOT WHERE YOU COME FROM. YOUR NOT YOUR RACE, HERITAGE, ETHNICITY, WHAT ANYONE'S SPOKEN ABOUT YOU, THE GEOGRAPHICAL AREA YOU LIVED. NONE OF IT. THE IDENTITY OF YOU IS SIMPLY A MATTER OF CHOICE AND WHAT YOU CHOOSE TO IDENTIFY WITH IN YOUR "HEART" (WHAT MAKES YOU YOU).

WHEN I WAS 17, I HAD ALMOST GOTTEN IN A LOT OF TROUBLE. PRISON. REAL TIME. NO DOUBT GOD'S GRACE THAT NOTHING HAPPENED. SOON AFTER I STARTED LOOKING AT MY LIFE AND WHO I WAS AND WHERE I WAS GOING. A FEW MONTHS AFTER, TOWARDS THE END OF A 3 MONTH ROAD TRIP WHILE VISITING A FAR AWAY TOWN, I RAN INTO SOME OLD FRIENDS AT A CONCERT. THEY INVITED ME TO GO TO COLORADO TO LIVE WITH THEM AND GET OUT OF THE SMALL TOWN WE CAME FROM. I DECLINED. 8 DAYS LATER I CAME HOME. I GOT A CALL FROM ONE OF THE GUYS AND AFTER TAKING A BRIEF LOOK AT MY LIFE I REALIZED I NEEDED A FRESH START IF I WAS GOING TO HAVE A CHANCE AT MAKING SOMETHING OUT OF MYSELF. I DECIDED TO GO. I TOLD MY MOM I

WAS LEAVING. PACKED MY STUFF AND HEADED OUT THE NEXT DAY. WHEN I LEFT, I SEVERED ALL CONTACTS WITH ANYTHING FROM MY PAST. UPON ARRIVING IN COLORADO, I TOOK A WALK UP IN THE MOUNTAINS OVERLOOKING BOULDER AND THOUGHT TO MYSELF "NOW WHAT?" "WHO AM I?" AS I BEGAN TO DISECT THAT, I REALIZED I HAD NO IDEA WHO I WAS. I CERTAINLY KNEW WHAT I WAS NOT. I DEFINITLY HATED THE WAY I DRESSED, MY HAIRCUT, THE WAY I TALKED, HAVING TO PRETEND I'M AN IDIOT (SO AS TO MAKE THE LOCALS WHERE I CAME FROM FEEL LESS THREATENED) THE WAY I WALKED (SLOUCHING AND FLOATING LIKE A STONER). THE MORE AND MORE I GOT INTROSPECTIVE I REALIZED I WAS LIVING OUT THROUGH A BARRAGE OF LAWS BASED OUT OF EVERYTHING EVERYONE SPOKE INTO AND OVER MY LIFE AND GETTING EXACTLY THOSE RESULTS. I EVEN HATED THE MUSIC I LISTENED TOO!

YOUR NOT THE THINGS THAT HAVE HAPPENED TO YOU, YOUR NOT WHAT PEOPLE HAVE SAID ABOUT YOU.

IDENTITY

ONE OF THE MORE ESCALATING PROBLEMS WE'RE CURRENTLY FACING TODAY IS THAT WE'RE LOSING OURSELVES...... ALL ACROSS THE WORLD INDIVIDUALISM IS BEING SACRIFICED TO "COOKIE CUTTER" IDEOLOGY. I'M WRITING THIS BOOK SITTING OVERSEAS IN EUROPE AND EVEN OVER HERE IM SEEING STRIP MALLS SLOWLY CREEP IN, FOOD CHAINS, MARKETPLACE CHAINS...

IN THE STATES I'M A HUGE FAN OF CHICAGO. NOT FOR THE REASON YOU'D THINK (BECAUSE IT'S HOME) BUT RATHER, BECAUSE WE DON'T GIVE AN ISH WHAT YOU THINK OR WHAT HAPPENS OUTSIDE OF CHICAGO. WE DO WHAT WE WANT.

I ONCE READ A FACEBOOK PAGE ENTITLED "YOU KNOW YOU'RE FROM CHICAGO WHEN" FOLLOWED BY ALL OF THESE STATEMENTS... "WHEN THIS AND WHEN THAT" ... ONE THAT PARTICULARLLY STOOD

OUT TO ME AT THE TIME, WAS "YOU KNOW YOU'RE FROM CHICAGO WHEN, YOU CAN DO WHATEVE'R YOU WANT AND NO ONE WILL STOP YOU" ... LOL IT'S SO TRUE... IT'S BECAUSE THE AUTHORITIES HAVE BIGGER FISH TO FRY THAN WORRY ABOUT YOU BOMBING (GRAFFITI ART) ON THE WALL NEXT TO THERE PATROL CAR WHILE THEY'RE SITTING IN IT (TRUE STORY) ... ;)

IN LIKE MANNER I TIP MY HAT TO BOSTON, & NEW YORK BECAUSE, THERE'S ONLY ONE. NO OTHER CITY LIKE IT. LOOKING AROUND, READING THE PAPERS, & WATCHING THE NEWS ON T.V., I SEE US SLOWLY LOSING OUR INDIVIDUALITY ON A STREET/MARKETPLACE LEVEL AS WELL AS US INDIVIDUALLY.

IT USED TO BE THAT EACH MAJOR CITY HAD A FLAVOR ALL ITS OWN AND YOU KNEW WHAT TO EXPECT IF YOU EVER WENT THERE... NOW LOOKING AROUND THERE'S A STARBUCK'S ON EVERY CORNER WITH A MCDONALDS ACROSS THE STREET AND THE BLASÉ ATTITUDES AND DEMEANOR OF THE LOCALS TO MATCH.

RESPONSIBILITY

MOST OF US HAD FATHERS THAT WERE NON-EXISTANT OR LESS THAN EXEMPLERY. SO. NO ONES GOING TO FIX YOU. IT'S UP TO YOU TO TAKE RESPONSIBILTY, MAN UP AND BE COUNTED. WE ALL GOT STUFF. FOR MOST OF US, CHILDHOOD WAS LONG AGO AND YOU CAN'T CHANGE THE PAST. THOUGH, YOU CAN CHANGE YOUR RESPONSE TO IT FOLLOWED BY YOUR FUTURE. GROW UP.

NOT SPEAKING AGAINST COUNSELORS, PSYCH DR'S, OR THERAPISTS. THEY ARE MUCH NEEDED. HOWEVER, THEY CAN'T BE WITH YOU 24/7. IT'S ALSO NOT YOUR SPOUSES, SIGNIFICANT OTHERS, PARENT'S, RELATIVES, OR DOG'S JOB.

IT'S NO ONES RESPONSIBILITY BUT YOUR OWN. IF YOU MADE THE CHOICE TO READ THIS BOOK WHETHER, IT WAS YOUR IDEA OR SOMEONE

TOLD YOU TO, AT SOME POINT YOU CHOSE TO ACT ON IT PROVING YOU HAVE A WILL. IF YOU HAVE A WILL THEN THE RESPONSIBILITY IS ON YOU TO CHANGE SOME THINGS. TO BE MASTER OF YOUR DOMAIN...

JONAH

MANY HAVE HEARD THE STORY OF JONAH GETTING SWALLOWED UP BY A WHALE. IF NOT, THE SHORT VERSION AND ONE INTERPRETATION IS THIS. THERE WAS THIS GUY NAMED JONAH. GOD SENT HIM ON A MISSION THAT HE ABSOLUTLY DID NOT WANT TO DO. HE WAS TOLD TO GO AND BE A MISSIONARY TO THESE PEOPLE HE DESPISED AND REVOLTED BECAUSE OF THEIR WAYS (BLATENT SINNERS). INSTEAD OF ACCEPTING HIS RESPONSIBILITY AND FACING THE IMPERFECTION THAT HE HATED IN THESE PEOPLE. HE RAN. HE RAN AS FAR AS HE POSSIBLY COULD IN THE OPPOSITE DIRECTION.

I'M SURE HE WAS PROBABLY THINKING "I'M GETTING THE F OUTTA HERE. SCREW THAT NONSENSE". IN THE PROCESS OF THIS LITTLE VENTURE, HE GOT SWALLOWED UP BY A WHALE.

WHILE IN THE STOMACH OF THE WHALE HE HAD TIME TO THINK. DURING HIS STAY THERE HIS SKIN WAS BLEACHED WHITE. GROWING QUICKLY BORED OF HIS CURRENT PREDICAMENT, REGRET OF HIS COURSE OF ACTION BEGAN TO SET IN. HE CHANGED HIS MIND, ASKED GOD FOR HELP AND SOON AFTER HE WAS SPIT FROM THE WHALE'S MOUTH UPON THE SHORE OF THE VERY PEOPLE HE RAN FROM. ATTITUDE FRESH, MIND CHANGED HE CONTINUED ON HIS TASK A NEW MAN. HOW DOES THAT STORY APPLY HERE? THE SIGN OF THE PROPHET JONAH IS A CHANGED LIFE. A LOT OF PEOPLE ARE RUNNING FROM IMPERFECTIONS, DARK PLACES, HIDDEN THINGS AND ARE UNWILLING TO FACE THINGS IN THEIR LIFE THAT THEY HATE.

IT'S TIME PEOPLE QUIT FCKNG AROUND & PUT SOMETHING IN MOTION. START DOING SOMETHING, GOING THROUGH, OR GOING OVER.

FOR FAR TOO LONG PEOPLE HAVE BEEN SIMPLY GETTING A TONIC FOR THEIR AILMENTS MAKING THEMSELVES FEEL BETTER BY LISTENING TO OR READING MATERIAL BY MOTIVATIONAL SPEAKERS, TALKING TO THEMSELVES IN FRONT OF THE MIRROR, OR DISTANCING THEMSELVES FAR FROM THAT DARK/HIDDEN THING OR THINGS

THEY HATE IN AN ATTEMPT FORGET. BAND-AIDS. SOME OF THAT HAS ITS PLACE, BUT IT'S TIME TO EXAMINE YOURSELF AND THE HANDICAPS IN YOUR LIFE. SOME HANDICAPS ARE LONG SINCE BURIED LEAVING PERSONALITY SCARS LIKE THE HUNCHBACK OF NOTRE DAME. FACE & DEAL WITH THEM AND EMERGE HAVING A CHANGED LIFE. DO THIS IN ORDER THAT YOU CAN FINALLY LIVE FREE AND ACCOMPLISH WHAT IT IS THAT YOU WANT TO DO WITHOUT BAGGAGE.

QUIT BLAMING PEOPLE FOR YOUR OWN ACTIONS. THAT'S SOME CRY BABY SH*T. ACCEPTING RESPONSIBILITY IS THE FIRST STEP TOWARDS BEING IN AUTHORITY. DON'T' BEND OVER AND TAKE IT LIKE SOME JELLYFISH. DO SOMETHING ABOUT IT(RESPONSIBLY)

FAITH

THE THING ABOUT FAITH IS THAT MOST PEOPLE ONLY SEE IT AS ONE SIDED. "HAVE FAITH IN GOD AND POSITIVE THINGS WILL HAPPEN" YADA, YADA, YADA... LOOK, IF THERE'S A GOD THEN THERE'S A DEVIL. IF THERE'S POSITIVE FAITH THEN THERE'S NEGATIVE FAITH.

YOU ARE WHAT YOU EAT. PAY ATTENTION TO WHAT YOU'RE THINKING.

I'M GOING TO NAME 3 THINGS. AS I SAY THEM, I WANT YOU TO PICTURE THEM IN YOUR MIND. READY?

PICTURE A TRAIN.

GOT IT? COOL.

NOW PICTURE A BUS.

NOW PICTURE A STOP SIGN.

NOW PAUSE A MINUTE AND THINK ABOUT THAT STOP SIGN. LET THE PICTURE RESONATE FOR 15 SECONDS.

NOW, DO YOU SEE HOW EASY IT IS TO CHANGE WHAT WERE THINKING ABOUT AND TO STOP THINKING ABOUT CERTAIN THINGS?

FOR THOSE OF YOU FAMILIAR WITH THE FAIRIED SWORD EXCABILER, EXCALIBER IS ALSO SYMBOLIC OF AND IN REFERANCE TO THE MIND. WERE NOT MEANT TO BE SUBECT TO OUR MIND BUT RATHER OUR MIND BE SUBJECT TO US. YOUR MIND IS THE KEY TO ALOT OF THINGS. IT'S A POINTMAN AS WELL AS A RUDDER. WE ARE TO BE IN CONTROL OF OUR MIND. WE ARE TO CONTROL OUR MIND, NOT IT CONTROL US. IT'S A TOOL. A DEVESTATING ONE. GOING BACK TO FAITH... WHERE THE MIND GOES THE MAN FOLLOWS, BECUASE, "AS A MAN THINKETH IN HIS OWN HEART SO IS HE". THE BIBLE SAYS TO "GUARD YOUR HEART FOR OUT OF IT FLOWS THE ISSUES OF YOUR LIFE". WHAT DOES THAT MEAN EXACTLY? YOU HAVE TO BE CAREFUL WHO AND WHAT YOU LET GET CLOSE TO YOU BECAUSE THEY HAVE DIRECT ACCESS AND INFLUENCE TO YOUR HEART. EVER WONDER WHY SIBLINGS CAN MAKE YOU INSTANTLY ANGRY? A PERSON OFF OF THE

STREET AND YOUR BROTHER OR SISTER CAN SAY THE EXACT SAME THING TO YOU BUT YOU ONLY FLIP OUT AT YOUR BROTHER AND SISTER, NOT CAREING AT ALL ABOUT THE OTHER GUY... IT'S BECAUSE OF THE PROXIMITY TO YOUR HEART...

YOUR MIND IS THE GUARD OR FILTER OF YOUR HEART. IT DETERMINES WHAT AFFECTS YOU AND WHAT DON'T. IT DETERMINES WHAT YOU CHOOSE TO BELIEVE AND WHAT YOU DON'T. THE PROCESS IS KINDA LIKE THIS. THINGS GO TO YOUR MIND AND THEN MAYBE OR MAYBE NOT DROP DOWN INTO YOUR HEART (WHAT MAKES YOU, YOU... YOUR LIFE). IF IT'S SOMETHING YOU CHOOSE TO RECEIVE IT'S AT THAT POINT A SEED. FOLLOWED BY SOMETHING ELSE THAT YOU CHOOSE TO BELIEVE AT SOME POINT, CONFIRMING WHAT YOU ALREADY CHOSE TO BELIEVE THUS, "WATERING" THAT INITIAL SEED OR THING. THEN, IT TAKES ROOT, (IN YOURT HEART) STARTING TO AFFECT HOW YOU INTERPRET THINGS OR YOUR PERSPECTIVE (YOUR FAITH OR WHAT YOU BELIEVE). NOW, SINCE YOUR "GUARD IS DOWN" REGARDING THAT THING, THE EASIER YOU'LL RECEIVE OTHER THINGS OF THAT NATURE AND THAT ROOT GETS WATERED MORE... THEN, ALONG THE WAY IT'LL GET TESTED BECAUSE WE'RE IN A HUGE WORLD FULL OF

PEOPLE WHO DON'T THINK LIKE US. AT THE POINT OF TESTING, WE MAKE THE DECISION TO OWN IT OR NOT(AUTHORITY) BY, CHOOSING TO REMAIN RESOLUTE. EITHER BY DEFENDING IT, HOLDING FAST, OR BUCKING AND YEILDING... AS THIS (THE PROCESS) IS NOW ALL BECOMING SECOND NATURE IN OUR SUBCONSCIOUS THROUGH REPETATIVE CONTESTING, WHAT HAPPENS THEN IS THE ROOTS GROW DEEPER BOTH IN OUR HEARTS AND PSYCHE. THESE ROOTS WILL EVENTUALLY PRODUCE FRUIT, WHICH MANIFESTS IN OUR LIFE BY OUR PERCEPTIONS, ATTITUDES, VIEWS, & DECISIONS. ALL OF WHICH TAKES PLACE IN THE MIND.

GOING BACK TO THE 2 FAITHS. WE ALL KNOW ABOUT FAITH. PEOPLE BELIEVE (HAVE FAITH) IN MANY THINGS. PEOPLE THINK THAT IF THEY BELIEVE, GOOD THINGS WILL HAPPEN, BUT NO ONE EVER CONSIDERS THE NEGATIVE SIDE OF THAT. LET'S TAKE FEAR FOR INSTANCE. FEAR IS SIMPLY THE COMPLETE OPPOSITE OF FAITH. HOWEVER, IT'S ACTUALLY STILL FAITH. IT'S "FAITH IN REVERSE" IF YOU WILL. NEGATIVE FAITH. OF THE TWO, FEAR IS ACTUALLY THE ONE WITH THE STRONGEST PULL OUT THERE BECAUSE WE'RE SO PRONE TO IT AS IT'S IN OUR NATURE. WHEN YOU DRIVE A CAR IT'S

ALL TOO COMMON AND IN FACT NATURAL (UNLESS YOUR TRAINED OTHERWISE) THAT WHEREVER YOU FOCUS ON YOU'LL HEAD THAT DIRECTION... OFF OF THE ROAD, INTO ONCOMING TRAFFIC, INTO POOR PEDESTRIANS. NO GOOD ALL THE WAY AROUND.... LOL. FAITH WORKS IN THIS SAME FASHION. WHATEVER YOU FOCUS ON YOU'LL HEAD DOWN THAT PATH AND EVEN BECOME(HITTING) WHATEVER IT IS YOUR STARING AT. (WELCOME TO FRONT STREET) SO, WHAT IS IT THAT YOUR STARING AT? NOW'S THE TIME TO TAKE A MOMENT. DOING SO REGULARLY IS GOOD. NECESSARY EVEN. TAKE 1 HOUR AWAY FROM ANYTHING FAMILIAR, TURN OFF THE CELL PHONE, REMOVE DISTRACTIONS. WHATEVER IT TAKES SO YOU CAN BE UNINTERRUPTED IN YOUR THOUGHTS BEING ABLE TO GIVE THEM TO THIS ONE THING. WHAT ARE OR HAVE YOU BEEN STARING AT? THE THINGS THAT HAVE BEEN SPOKEN OVER YOU? THE THINGS THAT HAVE HAPPENED TO YOU? THE ADOPTED BELIEFS, MINDSETS, AND NOTIONS OF EVERYWHERE YOU CAME FROM OR PASSED THROUGH? IF SO, THEN I GUARANTEE YOU WILL BECOME ALL OF THOSE THINGS REAPING THE WHIRLWINDS AND EFFECTS OF THEM UNLESS YOU DO SOMETHING TO CHANGE IT. IT'S NOT EASY. BUT IT GETS EASIER.

THE BRAIN IS A MUSCLE IF YOU WILL…. LIKE ANY MUSCLE, WORKING OUT TYPICALLY IS HARD AT FIRST BUT, IT GETS EASIER AND MORE NATURAL WITH TIME. YOU CAN BRAINWASH YOURSELF TO BELIEVE WHATEVER YOU WANT TO. GOOD OR BAD. LOOK AT A FEW PLACES AROUND THE WORLD WHEREIN THEY ARE MASTERS AT IT AND YOU'LL ALWAYS SEE CERTAIN KEY ELEMENTS OF THE PROCESS THE SAME IN EACH ORGANIZATION. NAMING TWO TO START, NO ONE IS BETTER AT IT THAN THE UNITED STATES MILITARY, (NOT THAT IT'S A BAD THING, I LOVE MY COUNTRY AND MY MILITARY) & THE SECOND BEING, THE THIRD REICH. WHAT DO THEY DO THAT THEY HAVE IN COMMON REGARDING THIS TOPIC? THEY CONSTANTLY BARRAGE YOU WITH WHAT THEY WANT YOU TO BELIEVE, THEY'LL BARRAGE YOU WITH MUCH MORE THAN WHAT YOU WOULD EVER WANT FOR SURE. SPEEDING UP THIS PROCESS DRAMATICALLY BY SLEEP DEPRIVATION, EXTREME PHYSICAL EXERTION, MEAL DEPRAVATION, TRAUMA OF ALL SORTS. ALL WHILE UNDERGOING CONSTANT BOMBARDMENT FROM ALL SIDES HONING WHAT IT IS THAT THEY WANT YOU TO BELIEVE, KNOWING THAT YOU WILL BECOME THAT AND THAT BECOMING SECOND

NATURE OR SUBCONSCIOSLY. IE. IF IN THE HEAT OF BATTLE, YOU ARE IN A CRITICAL POSITION WHERE YOU DONT HAVE TIME TO THINK ONLY REACT (SUBCONSCIOUS)...AND YOU HESITATE FOR ONLY A SECOND, YOUR POTENTIALLY DEAD ALONG WITH EVERYONE AND WHATEVER MISSION OBJECTIVE YOUR ON.

SO, TRAIN, BUS, STOP SIGN. ONCE YOU DETERMINE WHAT IT IS YOU WANT TO BECOME THAT DETERMINES THE DIRECTION. THINK ABOUT WHAT YOU ARE THINKING ABOUT. ANYTHING THAT IS OF THE 3 D'S, DOUBT, DEFEAT, OR DISCOURAGMENT IS ROOTED IN FEAR AND IS FROM THE DEVIL. EVEN IF YOU DON'T BELIEVE ALL THAT (THE DEVIL), THOSE THINGS ARE CERTAINLY NOT ANYTHING I WOULD WANT IN MY LIFE THAT'S FOR SURE... NOW WHAT? NOW THAT YOU'VE ISOLATED THE THOUGHT, YOU FIGURE OUT WHAT TO DO WITH IT. REAP IT OR KEEP IT. IT DEFINITLY SOUNDS CHEEZY BUT, IT'S A SYSTEM YOU'LL NEVER FORGET. IF IT'S SOMETHING TO GET RID OF OR THAT YOU'D RATHER NOT THINK ABOUT, CHANGE IT. CHANGE YOUR MIND. THINK THE EXACT OPPOSITE ABOUT THAT THING IF YOU WANT. THAT'S ALWAYS WORKED FOR ME. FEAR IS A LIE. THE ACRONYM (JOYCE MEYER I THINK).

F.E.A.R. FALSE. EVIDENCE. APPEARING. REAL. FEAR IS JUST A MASCARADE WAITING FOR YOU TO BITE SO HE CAN FEED YOU MORE SH*T AND CARRY YOUR LIFE AWAY. IF FEAR IS A LIE, THEN A GOOD PLACE TO START IS BY CHOOSING TO BELIEVE (CHANGING YOUR THOUGHT(S)) TO WHATEVER THE OPPOSITE IS OF WHAT YOU'RE AFRAID OF, (OR DOUBTING, DISCOURAGED, ETC. ETC.). MAYBE, WHATEVER YOU'RE CHOOSING TO BELIEVE IN THE BATTLE OVER YOUR MIND ISN'T EXACTLY ACCURATE EITHER... MEANING, YOU FEEL LIKE THE KING LOSER SO YOU CHOOSE TO BELIEVE THE OPPOSITE. THAT YOU'RE THE GREATEST MAN ON THE EARTH IN APPROPRIATE FASHION. OK? SO. WHAT'S WRONG WITH HOPE? ISN'T THE LATTER THOUGHT BETTER THAN THE FORMER THOUGHT? IF NOTHING ELSE, AT LEAST YOUR HEADED IN THE RIGHT DIRECTION... I'D PERSONALLY RATHER ERROR ON THE SIDE OF POSITIVE FAITH THAN NOT. EVEN IF YOU LEAN ON THE SIDE OF MEGALOMANIA. AT LEAST YOUR A STEP UP. WE ALREADY KNOW THAT FEAR WORKS. MOST OF US HAVE LIVED OUR WHOLE LIVES STRUGGLING WITH IT. WHATS WRONG WITH TRYING TO SEE IF FAITH WORKS? IF NOTHING ELSE, YOU'RE CREATING AN ATMOSPHERE IN & AROUND YOURSELF FOR

GROWTH BY RELACING THE NEGATIVE THOUGHTS. WHICH, BY DEFAULT.... LEADS TO BETTER THINGS HAPPENING AND YOUR LIFE BEING CHANGED BECUASE THE FRUIT IS CHANGING OUT OF YOUR HEART. I DON'T KNOW ABOUT YOU BUT I'VE HAD ENOUGH OF MY LIFE DOMINATED BY SH*T THAT DON'T HELP ME ONE BIT. IT'S A SHAME WE WERE NEVER TAUGHT HOW TO UTILIZE OUR MIND AS A TOOL FOR CRITICAL PERSONAL DEVELOPEMENT AS A KID... HOW DIFFERENT WE WOULD BE TODAY, I'M SURE.

AUTHORITY IS AS SIMPLE AS A DECISION. A CHOICE.

YOU WILL EVENTUALLY BECOME WHATEVER IT IS THAT YOU ARE LOOKING AT...THE ONLY PROBLEM WITH THAT IS, THAT THOSE OF YOU WHO CHOSE TO GO TO THOSE DARK PLACES IN LIFE....YOU MIGHT NOT FIND YOUR WAY BACK. TAKE A LOOK AT SOME METHOD ACTORS (THE ART OF GIVING YOURSELF TO THE PART IN ORDER TO BECOME THE PART FOR THE ROLE). SOME ROLES CHANGED THEM PERMENANTLY. BE CAREFUL WHAT IT IS THAT YOU GIVE YOURSELF TO LEST YOU FORGET WHO YOU ARE.

ALL CODE IS LEGACY CODE.

AGGRESSIVE FAITH

GOD CAN'T STEER A PARKED CAR. GOD CAN'T REALLY GUIDE YOU IF YOU'RE NOT MOVING ANYWHERE.

SOME THINGS YOU CAN ONLY START BY TAKING A STEP. SHAKY, & UNSURE IT DON'T MATTER. TAKE A STEP AND PURPOSE TO NOT QUIT. PICK A PACE YOU KNOW YOU CAN DO EVEN IF IT'S SLOW, & WALK... SOMETIMES, THAT'S ALL YOU CAN DO. SOMETIMES, ALL YOU CAN DO IS HOLD FAST AND STAND. JUST DON'T QUIT. SOMETIMES, IT TAKES BEING CREATIVE IN NEGOTIATING THE WATERS OF SITUATIONS IN ORDER TO MAKE ANY PROGRESS FORWARD. (NEVER TURN OFF YOUR BRAIN AND THINKING OUTSIDE THE BOX). NO PROBLEM... YOUR NOT IN A HURRY ANYWAY. CONSISTENCY

IS WHAT MATTERS NOT SPEED. BE SLOW AND PAY ATTENTION TO FORM. THERE'S ALL KINDS OF "MUSCLE MEMORY" IF YOU WILL... EMOTIONAL, MENTAL, LITERAL, SPIRITUAL, ETC... ONLY WORRY ABOUT NOT QUITTING FOLLOWED BY DOING IT RIGHT AND EVENTUALLY YOU WILL SUCCEED. "SLOW IS SMOOTH, SMOOTH IS FAST". CONSISTENCY IS HOW KINGDOMS DROP. THERE'S NOTHING WRONG WITH AGGRESSIVE FAITH. PUTTING THAT DEMAND ON GOD THAT SAYS "LOOK, I'M HERE. I'M GOING TO DO THIS. YOU'RE GOING TO NEED TO BACK ME UP OR I'M GONNA DIE IN DOING SO" ... THAT POINT WHEN YOU CHOOSE TO BELIEVE THAT GOD WILL GIVE YOU AN AREA SIMPLY BECAUSE YOU'RE YOU.... JOSHUA 1:3 IS PROBABLY MY PERSONAL FAVORITE AND THE PERSONAL TITLE SCRIPTURE FOR MY LIFE. IT STATES, "I WILL GIVE YOU EVERYWHERE YOUR FOOT TREADETH" THE PROBLEM IS THAT PEOPLE RARELY TAKE HIM AT HIS WORD. WHAT DO YOU HAVE TO LOSE? STEP OUT OF THE BOAT AND DON'T QUIT. WHAT'S THE WORST THAT CAN HAPPEN? YOU LOSE EVERYTHING AND FAIL?

HERE'S THE HARD NEWS. THAT'S PROBABLY GOING TO HAPPEN. IN FACT, I REALLY DON'T TRUST ANYONE THAT HASN'T FAILED OR HAD

HARDSHIP IN LIFE. WHY? BECAUSE THEY'VE NEVER BEEN ANYWHERE...THEY HAVE NO STORY TO TELL, NO MERIT TO THEIR CHARACTER. FAILING DEVELOPES THINGS IN YOU.

WHAT HAPPENS AFTER YOU FAIL? YOU MAKE SURE YOU LEARN FROM IT (THAT'S WHERE WISDOM COMES FROM) AND MOVE ONTO EITHER DOING IT AGAIN OR THE NEXT THING. (IE. BELIEVING SOMETHING JUST CAUSE, OR COMMANDING A DEMAND) (OBVIOUSLY, ALL IN ACCORDANCE WITH HIS WORD/WILL OR IT'S A PERSONAL IDOL AND/OR AGENDA AND THAT BEING SAID, SOMETHING IN VAIN) ANYONE WHO TELLS YOU ANYTHING DIFFERENT HAS NEVER DONE IT AND IS PROBABLY TO HUNG UP ON THEMSELVES AND THEIR AGENDA. PAY NO MIND TO THE NAYSAYERS, THE DEBBIE DOWNERS. ANYONE WHO ISN'T IN YOUR CORNER NOR, ON BOARD WITH WHATEVER IT IS YOUR RUNNING WITH. IN ORDER TO BREAK GROUND YOUR GONNA HAVE THAT. HAVE TO HAVE THAT, IN MY MIND. IT DEVELOPES TENACITY. SPARKS THE FIGHT IN YOU. I HAVE A HORRIBLE TRAIT. SOME CONSIDER IT A STRENGTH. PERSONALY, I'M STILL ON THE FENCE WITH THAT ONE... LOL. WHEN I SENSE THAT SOMEONE DON'T THINK I CAN DO SOMETHING, OR FEELS THAT

I CAN'T DO SOMETHING, OR DON'T WANT ME TO DO SOMETHING. I FEEL AS THOUGH THAT'S A CONFIRMATION THAT, THAT IS EXACTLY WHAT I'M SUPPOSED TO DO, &/OR I AM GOING TO DO. I'LL DIG MY HEELS IN. IF FOR NO OTHER REASON, JUST BECAUSE OF THEIR ATTITUDE. I PERSONALLY THRIVE ON CONFLICT (ANOTHER BAD TRAIT). GROWING UP I'D GO OUT OF MY WAY SIMPLY DO SOMETHING IN THE FACE OF WHAT OTHER'S BELIEVE, IF FOR NO OTHER REASON THAN TO CHANGE THEIR MIND, BREAKING THEIR MINDSET. TRUE INOVATION COMES FROM FLYING IN THE FACE OF ADVERSITY. THINKING BACK TO I THINK WHAT WAS AN OLD AD I SEEN YEARS AGO... "BREAK THE MOLD... CREATINE". SQUARE PEG DON'T FIT IN A ROUND HOLE? NO PROBLEM... THE THING ABOUT ROCKS IS WHEN THROWN IN A STREAM, RIVER ETC. THE WATER FLOWS AROUND IT. YOU DON'T HAVE TO BE WHAT EVERYONE WANTS YOU TO BE. DON'T MIND THEM AND CHANGE THE FLOW AROUND YOU.

WISDOM

GOD GAVE YOU A BRAIN.

USE IT.

FAITH WITHOUT WORKS IS DEAD.

MOUNTAIN TOPS

LENIN SAID ONCE, GIVE ME A GENERATION OF YOUTH AND I WILL CHANGE THE WORLD. THAT STATEMENT IS ENTIRELY TRUE. MOTHERS NURTURE, FATHERS DEFINE. IF YOU REMOVE OR HANDICAP THE INFLUENCE OF THE TRADITIONAL MALE ROLE MODEL YOU ASSASSINATE ONES CHARACTER AND/OR IDENTITY. I PERSONALLY BELIEVE THAT IS A DIRECT RESULT OF A LOT OF PROBLEMS IN SOCIETY WE HAVE TODAY.

THE ROLE OF THE FATHER HAS EITHER BEEN PHYSICALLY ELIMINATED, UNDERMINED, FEMINIZED, PENALIZED, PORTRAYED AS AN INFERIOR SPECIES WHO'S VOICE CARRIES NO REAL WEIGHT, INTEGRALLY PERVERTED WHETHER THROUGH SUBSTANCE ABUSE, UNETHICAL BEHAVIOR, ADULTRY, OR IMMORAL ACTS. THE DIRECT RESULT IS THAT YOU HAVE MULTIPLE

GENERATIONS OF PEOPLE FEELING EMPTY, WANDERING AROUND NOT KNOWING WHO THEY REALLY ARE ONLY LEFT WITH THIS HOLE. UNFULLFILLED, MISGUIDED, & MISLEAD THIRSTING TO FILL THIS VOID WITH SOMETHING. I BELIEVE THESE CURRENT AND PAST GENERATIONS ARE PROBABLY THE MOST PASSIONATE GENERATIONS TO EVER EXIST (LOOK AT THE X-GAMES). EVERYONE WANTS TO BELIEVE IN SOMETHING. I BELIEVE IT IS IN LARGE PART DUE TO THEM NOT HAVING A FATHER. THE MORE DESPERATE ONE BECOMES THE MORE PASSIONATE HIS VENTURE. PEOPLE WILL PURSUE THINGS TO THE END OF THE EARTH COUNTING ALL AS COST, EVEN DEATH IN THE ATTEMPT TO FEEL FULLFILLED... SATIATED...TO QUENCH THEIR SEARCH.

PEOPLE ARE LOOKING TO SUMMIT MOUNTAIN TOPS BECUASE NO ONE TOLD THEM IS OK TO ENJOY LIFE IN THE VALLEYS.

SOMETIMES YOU HAVE TO LOSE YOURSELF IN ORDER TO FIND YOURSELF. NOT THAT MOUNTAIN TOPS DON'T HAVE THEIR PLACE... BUT THERE'S NOT LIFE ON THE SUMMIT...LIFE IS IN THE VALLEY. SUMMIT'S ARE FOR DIRECTION.

I JUST MEAN THAT PEOPLE EVERYWHERE ARE FIENDISHLY ATTEMPTING TO FILL THE VOID OF

ACCEPTANCE. WHEN ALL THEY NEED TO KNOW IS THEY'RE LOVED AND/OR ACCEPTED.

THINKING OF THIS GUY I SAW RECENTLY IN CHINA... ENGAGED. SUPPOSED TO BE MARRIED THE NEXT DAY OR SOMETHING... HE TOOK A BET TO HANG OFF OF A SKYSCRAPER FOR A SMALL AMOUNT OF CASH IN ORDER TO PAY FOR HIS WEDDING AND TAKE CARE OF HIS MOM OR SO WE'RE TOLD. IN DOING SO THE SKYSCRAPER WAS TOO SLIPPERY TO MAINTAIN HIS GRIP. AFTER MULTIPLE QUICK ATTEMPTS, HE WASN'T ABLE TO CLIMB BACK UP FALLING 60 STORIES TO HIS DEATH... R.I.P. WU YONGNING... THERE WAS NO ONE IN HIS LIFE WHOM HE RESPECTED ENOUGH TO TELL HIM NO. NO ONE IN HIS LIFE THAT HE WOULD LISTEN TOO.

WHY ARE VALLEY'S NO LONGER HOME? WHY IS IT THAT PEOPLE ARE NO LONGER COMFORTABLE AND WANT TO RESIDE THERE?

THIS WHOLE THING ABOUT ONLY FEEDING OFF THE EXHILERATION OF MOUNTAINTOPS... IT'S NOT HEALTHY... IT'S A DEFICIENCY... THE BIGGEST PROBLEM WITH THAT DEFIENCIENCY IS THAT IT MAKES YOU NUMB AND YOU BECOME ADEPT TO IT REQUIRING BOTH PUSHING THINGS FURTHER AND FURTHER AND BECOMING ACCUSTOMED TO

A LEVEL OF FEAR BEYOND REASON AND SAFETY. WHEN YOUR NO LONGER AFRAID OF FEAR, BAD THINGS HAPPEN. FEAR KEEPS YOU ALIVE.

YEARS AGO, I READ ABOUT THIS TEST THAT WAS CONDUCTED. RATS WERE USED IN TESTING THE EFFECTS OF CRYSTAL METH... AFTER THE INITIAL DOSE OF CRYSTAL METH., THEY WERE GIVEN 2 CHOICES THEREAFTER. LEAVING THEM FREE TO CHOOSE CHOICE A TO THE LEFT OR CHOICE B TO THE RIGHT OR CHOICE C BOTH. CHOICE A WAS SIMPLY GOOD FOOD AND CHOICE B CRYSTAL METH. THEY CHOSE CRYSTAL METH EVERYTIME. EVENTUALLY THEY STARVED TO DEATH BECAUSE THAT'S ALL THAT THEY ATE.

ALL PEOPLE ARE FUNDAMENTALY THE SAME. JUST AS ALL DNA IS FUNDAMENTALY THE SAME. IT CAN BE ALTERED BUT FIRST IT NEEDS TO BE EXAMINED CLOSELY TO SEE WHAT YOU'RE WORKING WITH.

IN ORDER TO BECOME MORE YOU FIRST HAVE TO BECOME LESS. IN ORDER TO EFFECTIVELY INCREASE YOU MUST EFFECTIVELY DECREASE. YOU MUST CONTRACT IN ORDER TO EXPAND. EVERYTHING SHIP SHAPE, OR THE ENCUMBERMENT IS A RECIPE FOR CHAOS AND/OR DISASTER.

THERE'S A TIME TO BE HARD AND A TIME TO BE SOFT. IT IS PERTINANT THAT YOU ALLOW A CERTAIN AMOUNT OF HARD THINGS IN YOUR LIFE IN ORDER TO DEFINE YOU AND GIVE YOU THE ABILITY TO STAND, CUT, AND/OR PUSH THRU OBSTICALS UNWAIVERING. HOWEVER, ANY GOOD FIGHTER KNOWS THAT HE ALSO HAS TO BE SOFT IN ORDER TO BE HARD. IF YOUR NOT SOFT (LOOSE, RELAXED, MARGINALLY PLIABLE) YOU'LL NEVER BE FLUID OR EFFICIENT NOR HAVE ANY KIND OF STAMINA. IF YOUR ALWAYS TENSE IE. STRESSING, STRUGGLING, WORRIED, FULL OF FEAR, OR GRIEF, CARRYING AROUND THE BONDAGE/BAGGAGE OF TRYING TO BE WHAT YOUR NOT, YOU'LL ALWAYS BE WARRING AGAINST YOURSELF. YOU CAN'T BE FIGHTING YOURSELF AND TRYING TO TAKE GROUND. THAT'S ASININE. IN ORDER TO BE STREAMLINED, FOCUSED, & EFFICIENT, YOU NEED TO LAY THOSE THINGS DOWN THAT PLAY AGAINST YOU. THEN YOU'LL BE AN EFFECTIVE FIGHTER AND BE ABLE TO CONQUER BECUASE, YOUR NOT OUT OF BALANCE. EVERY GOOD BLADESMITH KNOWS THAT A GREAT BLADE CAN'T JUST BE HARD. IT HAS TO BE ABLE TO BEND A LITTLE. NOT ONLY JUST FLEX EITHER. WHILE ALSO, BEING WELL BALANCED AND FULL OF THE RIGHT CHARACTER ELEMENTS.

COMPETITION

LIFE IS HARD. ONCE YOU ACCEPT THAT YOU'LL BE ABLE TO MOVE FORWARD. MOST PEOPLE NEVER GET PAST THE "WHOA IS ME STAGE", LIVING IN A LIFELONG RUT. THINGS WILL ALWAYS BE COMING AT YOU. ALWAYS. DECIDING TO MAKE UP YOUR MIND REGARDING WHAT YOU DO WITH THAT WILL DETERMINE YOUR FUTURE. YOU HAVE TO ACCEPT THAT, THAT'S JUST WHATS GOING TO HAPPEN. NOT QUIT. JUST KEEP GOING AND ENJOY THE TIMES IN BETWEEN AND IF POSSIBLE, DURING. SAILBOATS CUT THRU THE WATER USING THE WIND PRESSING AGAINST THEM PROPELLING THEM FORWARD.

KINGS DON'T COMPETE. A TRUE KING ISN'T CONCERNED WITH EVERYONE ELSE. WHAT MAKES A KING A KING BEYOND INHERITANCE IS THAT HE'S THE BEST AT WHAT HE DOES. HE DOESN'T NEED

TO PROVE HIMSELF TO ANYONE. HE'S KING. KING'S ARENT' WORRIED ABOUT THE COMPETITION, WHO'S DOING WHAT, AND IF IT'S BETTER. THE MINUTE YOU COMPETE WITH SOMEONE YOU LOSE. HOW'S THAT? THE MINUTE YOU FALL INTO THE TRAP OF PRIDE, FEELING AS THOUGH YOU HAVE TO PROVE SOMETHING, YOU LOSE TO WHATEVER OR WHOMEVER... FEELING AFRAID OR INTIMIDATED? IT'S O.K. TO FEEL AFRAID, JUST MAKE SURE IT ABSOLUTELY DOES NOT MOTIVATE OR INITIATE ANY ACTION OR THOUGHTS ON YOUR PART. THE SECOND THAT HAPPENS, THAT PERSON OR SITUATION OWNS YOU. WHY? BECAUSE YOU WALK AWAY FROM AUTHORITY IN THE SITUATION BY YIELDING TO THAT (AND LETTING IT OVERTAKE YOU). YOU'LL NEVER BE IN AUTHORITY IF YOU YIELD TO FEAR, INSECURITY, MANIPULATION, CONTROL, PRIDE, ETC...

KINGS DO HOWEVER COMPETE WITH THEMSELVES. IF YOU'RE GOING TO BE KING YOU NEED TO GET USED TO BEING ALONE... OR FLYING SOLO AS NEEDED FROM TIME TO TIME. AS KING YOU NEED TO CONTINUE TO SET THE BAR AND BREAK IT. BUT, YOU NEED TO SET YOUR OWN BAR. CONQUER MOUNTAINS AND TEST LIMITS WHEN NO ONE IS WATCHING, WHERE YOU'LL

GET NO AWARDS OR ACCOLADES FOR IT. PRIDE WILL KILL YOU EVERYTIME. THERE'S NO ROOM FOR PRIDE IF YOU'RE THE ONLY COMPETITION (IN YOUR MINDSET). IF THAT'S ALL YOUR FOCUSED ON, THEN THERE'S NO TIME TO LOOK AROUND THE ROOM AND SEE WHERE YOUR AT. NO ROOM TO GET A BIG HEAD... OUTSIDE OF THAT, WHAT'S THE KEY TO BEING HUMBLE? REMEMBER WHERE YOU CAME FROM. FROM TIME TO TIME, I'LL EAT A MEAL THAT TAKES ME BACK... BOTH SHOWING HOMAGE AND IN ORDER TO REMEMBER WHERE I CAME FROM... I REMEMBER THE DAYS OF GOVN'T CHEESE, FREE TURKEY'S, KOOL-AID WITHOUT SUGAR, 2 DAY OLD WONDER BREAD, AND THE TWINKIE I HAD FOR MY 6TH BIRTHDAY WITH 1 (USED) CANDLE IN IT BECAUSE WE COULDN'T AFFORD ANYTHING ELSE...

WE ALL HAVE CERTAIN CARDS THAT HAVE BEEN DEALT TO US. WE CAN ONLY PLAY THOSE CARDS THE BEST WE CAN GIVEN OUR CURRENT KNOWLEDGE AND WHAT WE HAVE TO WORK WITH. DON'T BE IN A HURRY. THINGS WILL EVENTUALLY MOVE FASTER BUT MOST AREN'T READY FOR THEM YET. THE FASTER YOU MOVE, THE FASTER AND HARDER THE OBSTICALS COME AT AND HIT YOU. MOST ARENT ABLE TO TAKE THE HIT. SET

A PACE, EVEN IF IT'S A SLOW WALK. SET YOUR MIND TO NOT QUIT AND EVENTUALLY YOU'LL GET FASTER, STRONGER, & MORE PERCEPTIVE. THUS, ALLOWING YOU TO ANTICIPATE, PLAN, BE MORE RESILIANT, AND PUSH THRU BETTER. MOST PEOPLE ARE IN SUCH A HURRY TO COMPETE AND WIN THE RACE THEY DON'T REALIZE THEY'RE RUNNING AGAINST THEMSELVES. THE ADAGE OF KEEPING UP WITH THE JONES'S NOT REALIZING THAT THEY'RE ("THE JONES'S") ARE TRYING TO KEEP UP WITH YOU....

SUCCESS

SUCCESS MEANS DOING SOMETHING SINCERELY AND WHOLEHEARTEDLY (BEING TRU TO YOU AND YOUR MOTIVES) HOWEVER, BRUCE LEE SAID IT BETTER... "SUCCESS MEANS DOING SOMETHING SINCERELY AND WHOLEHEARTEDLY, AND YOU HAVE THE HELP OF OTHER PEOPLE TO ACHIEVE IT" SUCCESS ALWAYS ALLOWS ROOM TO TAKE PEOPLE WITH... THE OLD SAYING OF YOU GOTTA GIVE BACK...

CONFIDENCE IS ALSO KEY TO SUCCESS TO ANY AREA OF LIFE. CONFIDENCE CAN BE LEARNED LIKE ANYTHING ELSE.

A LOT OF PEOPLE ARE AFRAID OF BEING SUCCESSFUL AND OFTEN PURPOSEFULLY OR SUBCONSCIOUSLY SABATOGE IT. PEOPLE WILL SABATOGE THEIR JOBS, FINANCES, RELATIONSHIPS, EDUCATION, MATERIAL WEALTH, EVERYTHING.

THEY'LL DO IT OFTEN ON PURPOSE SO AS TO REMAIN IN CONTROL AND NOT BE SUCCESSFUL. IT'S A DEFENSE MECHANISM. IT'S UNCHARTED WATERS FOR THEM SO THEY ABORT ALLOWING THEM TO BE IN THEIR COMFORT ZONE.

FEAR CAUSES YOU TO DO 2 THINGS. FIGHT OR FLIGHT. THERE ARE SUB-CATAGORIES TO BOTH OF THOSE OF COURSE BUT CONTROL TYPICALLY FALLS UNDER THE FIGHT SIDE. FEAR IS THE ROOT OF CONTROL. SO, WHEN SUCCESS IS THERE, OR LOCKED IN SIGHT FOR A SURE WIN. THEY'LL EITHER TAKE CONTROL, MANIPULATE THINGS, OR EVADE THINGS BY QUITTING THEM ALL TOGETHER. ALL THIS BECAUSE IT'S UNCOMFORTABLE, OR IT'S WHAT WASN'T SPOKEN OF THEM OR BELIEVED ABOUT THEM. EVEN IF IT'S THEM BELIEVING IN THEMSELVES. BEING A LEPAR (FEELING SORRY FOR YOURSELF) HAS NO PLACE IN ANY SUCCESSFUL PERSON NOR THEIR FUTURE.

LIFE HAPPENS TO EVERYONE, IT'S WHAT YOU DO WITH IT AFTER THAT, THAT MATTERS.

HUMANS AS A WHOLE ARE RESISTANT TO CHANGE. BY NATURE, WE HAVE TO PURPOSE TO CHANGE THINGS. EVEN THEN IT'S HARD. WE LIKE OUR NESTS...

LIFE IS SHORT, GOES BY ALL TOO QUICK. CARPE DIEM. DO SOMETHING DIFFERENT AND EMBRACE WHATS YOURS.

DOMINION

YOU CAN ONLY CONTROL SO MUCH...LIFE IS REALLY ONLY ABOUT OUR REACTION TO IT. I HAVE THIS SPACE 2 FEET IN FRONT OF ME 2 FEET ON BOTH SIDES AND 2 FEET BEHIND ME... ENTER THIS SPACE AND WE GOT PROBLEMS. ARE YOU A PRODUCT OF YOUR ENVIRONMENT OR IS YOUR ENVIRONMENT A PRODUCT OF YOU?

YEARS AGO, I STAYED AT A FRIEND'S HOUSE WHILE WAITING FOR AN APARTMENT TO OPEN UP. HE WASN'T MUCH OF A HANDYMAN NOR WAS ANY OF THE 3 OTHER GUYS LIVING THERE... I AM THE KINDA GUY WHO REALLY DOESN'T GIVE AN ISH IF YOU LIKE WHAT I'M DOING OR NOT. KEEPING IN MIND THIS ISN'T MY HOUSE... I STARTED THROWING THINGS OUT, PUTTING NAILS IN AND PULLING THEM OUT OF STUFF, MOWING THE LAWN WEEKLY AND IN OPPOSITE DIRECTIONS,

TRIMMING, PULLING WEEDS, CUTTING BRANCHES DOWN IN THE BACK YARD. CLEANING THE GARBAGE CANS. FIXING ISH. MAKING THINGS AS PRESENTABLE AS WHAT I HAD TO WORK WITH. ONE DAY ONE OF THE NEIGHBORS CAME UP AND SAUGHT ME OUT IN THE BACK YARD. HE, WHILE WALKING UP TO SHAKE MY HAND SAID... I'M NOT SURE WHO YOU ARE OR WHAT HAPPENED BUT, AS SOON AS YOU MOVED IN HERE THE WHOLE AREA CHANGED. IN ORDER TO BE IN AUTHORITY OF ANY SITUATION YOU FIRST HAVE TO OWN IT...

WHATEVER YOU DO IN LIFE, OWN IT. MAKE IT YOURS. THAT'S WHO YOU ARE. WHATEVER YOU DO, WHATEVER YOU THINK, WHATEVER YOU SAY, THAT'S YOU. IT DOESN'T MATTER HOW BIG, OR SMALL. WHATEVER HAND YOU'VE BEEN DEALT, OWN IT. TAKE CONTROL AND ACCEPT RESPONSIBILITY FOR IT. ONLY AFTER THAT, WILL YOU BECOME A BOSS.

OWNERSHIP = INVESTMENT. IN ORDER TO HAVE OWNERSHIP IN SOMETHING, THAT TAKES A COMMITTED INVESTMENT ON YOUR END. YOU HAVE TO BE ALL IN, IN WHATEVER YOU DO.

DECEITFUL URSURPERS RARELY LAST LONG. KINGSHIP CAN'T BE FAKED. IT HAS TO PERMEATE. SOMETIMES, IN ORDER TO CARRY A NEW MANTLE THINGS NEED TO BE LET GO OF IN ORDER FOR

TRANSFORMATION TO OCCUR. THAT'S THE SAME REASON REAR VIEW MIRRORS ARE SMALL AND WINDSHIELDS ARE BIG...

GOING BACK TO DECEITFUL URSUPERS, IF IT'S NOT REAL, THAT PERSON WILL WASH OUT EVERYTIME. ANY GOOD CHARLETAN CAN BUY TIME. SOMETIMES, EVEN ENOUGH TIME TO FINALLY REALLY CATCH UP TO WHAT HE'S PRETENDING TO BE TO BEGIN WITH... "FAKE IT TIL YOU MAKE IT". HOWEVER, EVEN THOSE PEOPLE STILL UNKNOWINGLY GO THROUGH THE PROCESS OF BEING TESTED (TO A DEGREE). WHEN YOU LEARN, YOU GET TESTED. THAT'S THE NATURAL ORDER OF THINGS. SO, EVEN AS THEY'RE FAKING IT, THEY'RE LEARNING AND BEING TESTED SIMPLY BY CHOOSING TO STAY THE COURSE.

THIS IS ALL SEASONAL, AS ALL OF LIFE IS SEASONAL.

IT'S VITAL TO KNOW WHAT DA WEATHER IS DOING. WHAT'S THE FORECAST? WHAT'S IT LOOKING LIKE OUTSIDE. WHERE YOU BEEN? HOW YOU NEGOTIATE THE WATERS OF THIS LIFE IS SOLELY DEPENDANT ON THAT. KNOWING WHAT TIME IT IS. THERE IS A SEASON FOR EVERYTHING.

SOME COATS ARE ONLY MEANT FOR A SEASON. THAT DOESN'T MEAN YOU LOSE THEM THOUGH...

AND THEN THERE ARE SOME COATS THAT GO UP IN RANK.

NOT REALIZING THAT YOU GRADUATED COULD STEAL YOUR NEXT BLESSING OR PROMOTION. KNOWING WHAT'S GOING ON WITH YOU & WITH THE ATMOSPHERE AROUND YOU, MAKES YOU AWARE OF HOW TO PREPARE AND WHAT TO DO. IF YOU DON'T KNOW OR ARE UNAWARE THAT IT'S TIME TO DO SOMETHING ELSE AND YOU'RE STILL LOOKING BACK FIXATED ON WHATEVER IT IS THAT YOU JUST WENT THROUGH, EXPERIENCED, TRAINED FOR OR MASTERED, YOU'LL HIT THE NEW SEASON UNPREPARED. EITHER, CAUSING YOU TO FLUB IT UP MISSING IT ALTOGETHER, STAY LONGER THEN NECESSARY, OR GO COMPLETELY BACK AROUND DOING IT OVER AGAIN. IF YOU MISSED IT, SOME WINDOWS ONLY HAPPEN ONCE... GOD CAN BRING THEM BACK AGAIN BUT, SOMETIMES THAT'S SIMPLY NOT IN THE WORKS. THAT'S WHY IT'S SO IMPORTANT TO ACCURATELY JUDGE WHAT'S UP. WE ALL WANT TO GET TO WHEREVER IT IS WE ARE GOING AS FAST AS POSSIBLE.

YOUTH & THE CHURCH

I FIND IT INTERESTING THAT THE TERM "ATOM" IS IN PARALELLE IN MANY WAYS TO "ADAM"(AS IN ADAM & EVE). IN PHONETIC'S, AND BOTH ARE IN ESSENSE THE ESSENCE OF ALL LIFE, OR THE BEGINNING, (LIFE IN THE RAW).

LIKE THE TWO, YOUTH ALSO ARE IN FACT THE BEGINNING OF LIFE.

UNSTRUCTURED, UNHARNESSED AND UNDISCIPLINED, YOUNG ENERGY... LIKE AN ATOM.... UNHARNESSED AND UNGUIDED BOUNCES ABOUT JUST CREATING FRICTION....

BUT IN THE SAME MANNER A NUCLEAR ATOM, GIVEN A CONTROLLED FORUM USING THE HARNESSED ENERGY IT ALTERS, RADIATES, CURES, AND AFTER BEING BROKEN, BECOMES THE MOST

EXPLOSIVE ENTITY KNOWN TO MAN, ALTOGETHER DEVASTATING THE WORLD FOREVER.

WHEN JESUS WALKED THE EARTH JOHN 6:1-15 STATES THAT IN SHORT.... JESUS USED THE SUBMITTED RAW ENERGY OF YOUTH TO GIVE LIFE TO THE MASSES.

ATOM=DNA, WHICH IS THE SUBSTANCE OF WHAT LIFE IS MADE OF. IT IS, IN SHORT, THE SUBSTANCE OF LIFE IN EVERYBODY. ALL THROUGH THE WORD ARE EXAMPLES THAT WE CAN JUDGE THE UNSEEN BY THE THINGS THAT ARE SEEN, SO AS IT WOULD APPLY IN SHORT.... YOUTH IS THE SUBSTANCE OF LIFE/ENERGY IN THE BODY (BODY OF CHRIST)

...ETC...

PRAYER

THE THING ABOUT PRAYER IS THAT YOU NEED TO PRAY CONVINCED. MOST PEOPLE THROW STUFF OUT THERE HOPING THE WIND BRINGS IT BACK (IN THE FORM OF AN ANSWER) ... LOL. NO. TRY THIS FOR A SEC... WHEN YOU PRAY, PRAY EXPECTING RESULTS. WHY? WELL... WHY NOT? GOD'S A GOD OF ANSWER'S, NOT CONFUSION. GOD'S ALL ABOUT BUILDING YOUR FAITH AND RELATIONSHIP WITH HIM... TRY HIM. "MY EYES ARE SEARCHING TO AND FRO TO FIND THOSE WHOM I MIGHT SHOW MYSELF FAITHFUL" ... AND "TASTE AND SEE THAT THE LORD GOD IS GOOD" TO NAME BUT A COUPLE OF SCRIPTURES ENFORCING THIS TRUTH.

SOME OF Y'ALL CAN'T QUIT. YOUR VISION IS SIMPLY TOO BIG. IF YOU QUIT IT WILL EAT YOU UP. JUST MOVE FORWARD ONE STEP AT A TIME. EVERYONE FLAILS AT FIRST, USUALLY MORE THAN

ONCE. IT'S THROUGH THE PROCESS OF FLAILING THAT WE GET OUR WINGS. CUT OUR TEETH. LOOK AT EAGLE'S FROM TIME TO TIME... SOMETIMES, THE PARENT EAGLE DROPS THE BABY EAGLE FROM UPON HIGH ONLY TO HAVE TO SWOOP DOWN AND SAVE HIM FROM SPATTERING ALL OVER... ONLY TO REPEAT THIS OVER AND OVER UNTIL THE BIRD GETS IT AND FLIES...

COMMIT FEARLESSEY & FEAR NOT. IT'S OK TO FEEL AFRAID, JUST DON'T LET IT MOTIVATE YOU. EMOTION IS NOT AUTHORITY. YOUR NOT IN AUTHORITY OVER ANYTHING IF YOUR NOT IN CONTROL OVER YOUR OWN MIND ("TRAIN, BUS, STOP SIGN"). YOU'LL NEVER BE A KING OR AT LEAST NOT VERY LONG IF YOU'RE NOT WALKING IN AUTHORITY. JUMP IN WITH BOTH FEET, FEARING NOTHING. MISTAKES WILL HAPPEN BUT THAT'S HOW YOU LEARN... STRAY FAR, FAR AWAY FROM THE PERSON WHO JUST SEEMS TO HAVE IT ALL TOGETHER...FOR THEY RARELY GET TESTED.

YOUR EMOTIONS ARE SUBJECT TO YOUR MIND. I GET THAT WOMEN ARE WIRED A LITTLE DIFFERENT THAN MEN SO THAT CONCEPT IS INTRINSICALLY MORE DIFFICULT TO CULTIVATE FOR THEM. WOMEN ARE BASICALLY WIRED ON EMOTION. THAT'S WHAT MAKES THEM SUCH

GOOD EMPATHIZERS. THEY. FEEL. EVERYTHING. BUT THE PRINCIPLE STILL APPLIES NONETHELESS.

HERE'S A VIRTUE...THIS ONES ALWAYS BEEN A PET PEAVE OF MINE. SOMETIMES YOU JUST NEED TO KEEP YOUR MOUTH SHUT. BEING TRUSTED IS KINDA LIKE GRAVITY... ONCE IT IS THAT YOU MAKE UP YOUR MIND TO MIND YOUR OWN BUSINESS AND KEEP YOUR MOUTH SHUT, THEN IT'S AS THOUGH YOU TURNED SOME KIND OF COSMIC KEY AND INFORMATION BEGINS TO FLOW STRAIGHT TO YOU.

THERE ARE FAR TOO MANY PEOPLE NAME DROPPING, PLACE DROPPING, DROPPING EVERYTHING IT SEEMS IN ORDER TO GET NOTICED AND FEEL IMPORTANT... HERE'S AN IDEA... TRY UNDERSTANDING THAT YOU DO CARRY WEIGHT (AS WE ESTABLISHED THAT EARLIER...THE PIECE IN THE PUZZLE... EQUALLY IMPORTANT...) AND THEN YOU DON'T HAVE TO TALK ABOUT YOURSELF ALL DAY. NO ONE REALLY CARES TO HEAR THAT STUFF ANYWAY, IN THE SAME MANNER POLES ON MAGNETS REPEL. THAT TOO IS LIKE GRAVITY... ONCE IT IS THAT YOU DON'T CARE TO BE HEARD, PEOPLE WILL WANT TO LISTEN. ONLY GOING FORWARD, QUALIFY WHAT IT IS THAT YOU HAVE TO SAY (THE PLACE OF KINGSHIP). MAKE IT COUNT.

YOU COULD ALWAYS GO A STEP FURTHER. NOW THAT YOUR COMFORTABLE WITH YOURSELF AND NOT NEEDING RECOGNITION, YOU COULD PAY IT BACK BY PAYING ATTENTION TO PEOPLE WITH A LITTLE SINCERITY AND SEE WHAT THAT DOES FOR YA... THE FURTHER YOU GET AWAY FROM YOURSELF AND COME TO THE END OF YOURSELF, THAT'S WHEN YOU START TO FIND THIS WHOLE OTHER LIFE OUT THERE. PICTURE A SLIDE BAR WHERIN ON ONE SIDE IT'S YOU AND YOUR POMPUS SELF, AND ON THE OPPOSITE SIDE IS OTHER PEOPLE AND RELATIONSHIPS. THE MORE YOU TEST THE WATERS AND SLIDE THE BAR, THE MORE THIS OTHER LIFE OPENS UP WITH OTHER PEOPLE AND FRIENDS WHO ACTUALLY LIKE YOU FOR YOU. BUT FIRST, FIRST YOU HAVE TO ACCEPT YOURSELF AND YOUR CODE.

NO ONE LIKES A POSER... YA, I KNOW... "ACT AS IF, RIGHT?" ACT AS IF, YOU'RE DA BOSS... YOUR DA KING SH*T... YOUR WELL ENDOWED... YOUR UBER EDUCATED... ETC... THAT'S ALL A BUNCH OF CRAP REALLY ANYWAY...

NO ONE LIKES STOLEN VALOR... IT'S EXCESSIVELY DISTASTEFUL AND EVEN AGAINST THE LAW IN SOME CASES... IE. MILITARY. THAT'S RIGHT, IT'S AGAINST THE LAW (FEDERAL) TO ASSUME SERVICE AND/

OR RANK YOU DIDN'T EARN. WALK AROUND ANY 1% CLUB OR ANY CLUB FOR THAT MATTER WITH A CUT ON THAT'S FAKE OR THAT YOU DIDN'T EARN. I GUARANTEE IT WILL BE TAKEN FROM YOU AT THE VERY LEAST...

IN ORDER TO BE GOOD AT ANYTHING, YOU HAVE TO CUT AWAY ALL THE BULLSH*T. WHATEVER IS GETTING IN THE WAY OF YOUR GOAL/PASSION. AT TIMES, AND GOOD GOD, I HOPE IT NEVER HAPPENS TO ANY OF YOU, WHEN SKYDIVING YOU HAVE A PROBLEM WITH YOUR MAIN(CANOPY). SOMETHING IS MALFUNCTIONING, AND IT'S GOING TO GET IN YOUR WAY AND/OR SERIOUSLY IMPEDE YOUR LANDING TO THE POINT OF A QUICK DEATH. IN ORDER TO PULL YOUR RESERVE AND CONTINUE ON IN SAFETY YOU'LL NEED TO PULL YOUR RELEASE AND CUT-AWAY YOUR MAIN & THERIN RELEASING YOUR RESERVE. BEING A POSER IS A LOT LIKE THIS. SOMETIMES, YOU HAVE TO BE WILLING TO FACE REALITY, CUT-AWAY THE GARBAGE IN ORDER TO SAVE YOUR LIFE. IT'S HARD TO FIGHT A BATTLE ON MORE THAN ONE FRONT FOR ANY AMOUNT OF TIME... ONCE YOU STOP BEING A POSER AND FULL OF CRAP THEN, YOU'LL HAVE ALL THIS EXTRA TIME, FOCUS, ENERGY TOWARDS ACTUALLY BECOMING WHATEVER IT IS THAT YOUR FAKING

BEING ANYWAY... WANT TO SPEAK 7 LANGUAGES? NO PROBLEM. QUIT COMPETING.

NOTHING IS TOO HARD. YOUR JUST TRAINED TO THINK IT IS. THINGS MAY MOVE SLOW AT FIRST BUT THE BRAIN IS LIKE A MUSCLE. IT JUST NEEDS RE-TRAINED AND CONDITIONED.

THE BRAIN IS A TOOL. ITS SOLE PURPOSE IS TO BE THERE FOR YOU TO USE. IT'S NOT GOING TO BREAK. YOU'RE NOT GOING TO ABUSE IT. IT'S THE MOST POWERFUL WEAPON ON THE PLANET YET, WE LET IT SLEEP IDLE, NEVER EXPLORING ITS FULL CAPABILITIES WHILE NEVER GIVING IT A SECOND THOUGHT. IT TAKES A CONSCIOUS EFFORT HONING, DEVELOPING, AND RE-DEVELOPING AN ELITE WEAPON.

CRÈME RISES TO THE TOP

"THE MORE YOU GET PUSHED, THE THICKER THE SKIN GETS, THE THICKER THE SKIN GETS THE HIGHER YOU GO" -GORDON RAMSAY.

CRÈME RISES TO THE TOP AS THEY SAY ONLY AFTER GETTING WHIPPED & BEAT DOWN A BIT.

ALL OF LIFE IS ABOUT HONING. A NEARLY CONSTANT STATE OF HONEING WITH "COOL DOWN" PERIODS IN BETWEEN SUBMISSION'S TO POUNDING, FIRE AND MOLDING (PUSHING & ARTICULATING A MASS).

YOU MAY NOT READ THE BIBLE OR THAT'S SIMPLY NOT YOUR THING. I DO FROM TIME TO TIME. LOL. SELF ADMITTADLY NOT AS OFTEN AS I SHOULD... IN IT WE'RE OFTEN REFERRED TO AS

CLAY, IRON, GOLD, ETC. THINGS THAT ARE SHAPED OR HONED.

TESTING HELPS YOU TO KNOW WHO YOU ARE.

WHAT DO YOU DO IN THE FACE OF ADVERSITY (ADVERSITY HAS MANY FORMS) DO YOU RUN AND COWER AS THOUGH, YOUR LIGHT IN THE WRIST? OR DO YOU FACE IT AND ATTEMPT TO DEAL WITH IT AS BEST YOU CAN EVEN IF YOU FAIL? FAILING IS NOT REALLY FAILING, IT'S JUST PRACTICE AND IT GET'S EASIER EVERY TIME. DON'T BE AFRAID OF CHALLENGES. THEY'RE REALLY SIMPLY PROMOTIONS IN HIDING. TESTING HELPS YOU TO KNOW WHO YOU ARE. WHEN CHOOSING TO DO SOMETHING AND STICKING TO IT IN SPITE OF. (FILL IN THE BLANK), YOUR DEVELOPING CHARACTER OR THICKER SKIN. WITH THAT COMES A MORE STABLE MINDSET. YOU DON'T GET PUSHED AROUND BY THINGS SO MUCH. YOUR NOT AS INTIMIDATED. AS THE PROCESS CONTINUES YOU BECOME MORE AND MORE AWARE OF YOUR LIMITATIONS. MOST PEOPLE ARE REALLY ONLY AFRAID OF THEMSELVES AND THEY DON'T EVEN KNOW IT. WHEN A FIGHT SURFACES, MOST PEOPLE ARE NERVOUS BECAUSE, THEY DON'T KNOW WHAT'S GOING TO HAPPEN. 90% OF THE TIME IT'S BECAUSE THEY DON'T KNOW THEIR LIMITATIONS.

HOW THEY CAN PERFORM. WHAT THEY CAN TAKE. ONCE THAT IS ELIMINATED, OR YOU BECOME MORE FAMILIAR WITH IT(YOU), NERVOUSNESS IS SIMPLY AN EMOTION THAT NO LONGER HAS A PLACE IT ONCE DID ALLOWING YOU TO FOCUS UN-INHIBITED ON THE ISSUE BEFORE YOU. THE PROCESS GROWS AS YOU KEEP STICKING TO CHOICES. WITH EACH PERSON IT'S DIFFERENT. THE CHOICES ARE OFTEN INTERNAL. THE BEST WAY IS TO MAKE A DECISION TO DO SOMETHING, STICK TO IT AND CONTINUE DOING SO THE REST OF YOUR LIFE.

IN TRANSIT

I NEVER WALK INTO A ROOM I DON'T KNOW HOW
TO GET OUT OF. I THINK THAT LIFE SHOULD BE
LIVED LIKE THIS. YOU SHOULD ALWAYS LOOK
AND THINK AHEAD. LOOK AND THINK ABOUT
HOW THINGS COULD PLAY OUT "IF" AND HAVE
A PLAN FOR IT. IT'S ALWAYS BEST TO THINK IN
TERMS OF CONTINGENCY PLANS... LOOSE ONES
FOCUSING ON THE MAJOR ISSUES/THREATS FIRST,
WORRING ABOUT THE MINOR THINGS NEXT. YET,
ALL THE WHILE ALLOW YOUR THINKING, REACTING,
DECISION MAKING TO BE PLIABLE AND ADENDUM'S
TO BE MADE AS NEEDED. SOMETIME'S, YOU ONLY
HAVE WHAT YOU HAVE TO WORK WITH NOW AND
EVEN THAT'S NOT SECURE. IT'S WHAT'S CALLED
AS BEING IN TRANSIT. I THINK THAT EVERYONE
SHOULD LEARN TO PLAY CHESS AS KIDS AND
PLAY AT LEAST SEMI-REGULARLY ALL OF THEIR

YEARS. IT KEEPS YOU SHARP WHILE TEACHING YOU HOW TO THINK, HOW TO STRATEGIZE, AND EFFECTIVELY DEAL WITH SITUATIONS AND POTENTIAL ANOMALIES DURING AND BEFORE THEY EVEN HAPPEN. MOST PEOPLE DON'T KNOW HOW TO THINK ANY MORE. ONLY LIVING FOR THE MOMENT. WHEN IN FACT YOU NEED BOTH. IT'S OK TO LIVE FOR THE MOMENT. WHEN TAKING GROUND, YOU OFTEN TIMES HAVE TO. BUT A PERSON IS AT A SERIOUS DISADVANTAGE IF HE'S NOT IN CONTROL OF HIS THINKING. YOUR MIND IS A TOOL. YOU CAN TRAIN YOUR MIND TO WORK FOR YOU LIKE ANYTHING ELSE. MUSCLE MEMORY FOR WEAPONS USE, COMBAT WHETHER HAND TO HAND OR TRAINING EXCERCISES ARE ALL A RESULT OF THE SAME PROCESS. TRAIN YOUR MIND TO WORK EFFECTIVELY FOR YOU WITHOUT THINKING ABOUT IT. IT SHOULD BE SECOND NATURE. IT'S SIMPLY HONED AND FORMED TO ARTICULATE CERTAIN PROCESSES ENABLING YOU TO BE FREE TO THINK ON THE FLY, CALMLY WITHOUT BURDEN. THUS, ALLOWING YOU TO THINK FREELY AND CLEARLY ON THE MATTER'S AT HAND.

SUCCESS IS A JOURNEY NOT A DESTINATION. DON'T BE IN A HURRY. RELAX IN YOUR OWN SKIN AND ENJOY THE RIDE... IT'S NOT ABOUT

MOUNTAIN TOPS IT'S ABOUT VALLEYS. VALLEY'S ARE DESIGNED FOR REFLECTION. THINKING ABOUT WHERE YOU'VE BEEN AND THE PINNACLE'S OF YOUR LIFE.

HUMILITY

NOT BEING PRIDEFUL IS INTRICATE IN FINDING SELF AND TRU-SUCCESS. THE ANTITHESIS OF PRIDE IS HUMILITY. YEP, I KNOW. THAT'S A FOREIGN WORD TO SOME... FOR MOST OF US WE'RE ALREADY THINKING OF SOMEONE WHO NEEDS IT. BUT NOT US RIGHT?

THE KEY TO HUMILITY IS ALWAYS REMEMBERING WHERE YOU COME FROM. NO ONE IS BETTER THAN ANYONE, WE JUST HAVE DIFFERENT POSITIONS. "EVERY JOB IS PRESTIGIOUS, WE JUST HAVE TO BE HUMBLE" -FERNANDO I FRATELLI DELIVERY DRIVER

ONE OF THE GREATEST THINGS ABOUT JUI JITSU IS THE MAT. THE MAT IS LIKE THIS GREAT EQUALIZER. WHEN YOU STEP OUT ONTO THE MAT EVERYONE IS EQUAL. SOCIAL STATUS, WEALTH, EVERYTHING OUTSIDE OF THE RAW YOU, HAS TO CHECK ITSELF AT THE DOOR.

DON'T GET IT TWISTED THOUGH...

BEING HUMBLE DOES NOT MEAN THAT YOU'RE A DOOR MAT. IT'S NOT OK TO CONSTANTLY LET PEAPLE WALK ALL OVER YOU, TREATING YOU LIKE GARBAGE.

RESPECT

I BELIEVE THAT EVERYONE HAS THE RIGHT OF BEING RESPECTED UNTIL THEY SHOW ME THAT THEY DON'T HAVE THAT RIGHT. I AM NOT SAYING THAT IF SOMEONE DISRESPECTS YOU THEN YOU INSTANTLY CHECK EM' AND SET THEM STRAIGHT USING WHATEVER MEASURE SEEMS FIT. KEEP IN MIND THAT SOME PEAPLE HAVE NEVER KNOWN RESPECT OR RATHER HAVE NEVER GOTTEN ANY. YOU CANNOT GIVE SOMETHING YOU DON'T HAVE. OFTEN TIMES YOU CAN DISARM SOMEONE BY GIVING THEM SOMETHING THEY LACK.

SOMETIMES (EVERYTIME ACTUALLY) WHEN YOU BELIEVE IN PEAPLE YOU CREATE A CAPACITY FOR THEM TO GROW/CHANGE. MEN BEING MEN ARE INNATELY PRE-DISPOSED TO REACTING TO RESPECT (OR LACK THEROF). WE VALUE THAT MORE THAN FEELINGS OR HEARTFELT MOMENTS.

TRY PUSHING PAST THE INITIAL BLOW BACK YOU GET FROM SOME PEAPLE CONTINUING TO SHOW THEM RESPECT AND THEY USUALLY UPON SENSING THIS WILL AUTOMATICALLY RECIPROCATE. MEN, (EVERYONE FOR THAT MATTER) JUST WANT TO FEEL RESPECTED AS INDIVIUALS. WE ARE HOWEVER, CREATED IN THE IMAGE OF GOD. HE COMMANDS RESPECT EVEN. "IF YOU DON'T PRAISE (SHOW RESPECT AND GRATITUDE) ME EVEN THE ROCKS WILL CRY OUT". NOT AT ALL SAYING WE NEED TO WORSHIP ONE ANOTHER. LOL. I'M SIMPLY STATEING RESPECT THE FREEDOM FOR ONE'S IDEAS, EXPERIENCES, AND CHOICES.

MOST OF THIS IS TIP OF THE ICEBURG STUFF, SO YOU CAN RUN WITH IT HOWEVER FAR YOU WANT...

A LOT OF THIS STUFF IS NOT ROCKET SCIENCE... SOMETIMES YOU JUST NEED TO HEAR IT FROM SOMEONE ELSE.

THE TERMINAL

THE DAY YOU STOP DREAMING IS THE DAY YOU BECOME OLD.

SOME OLD SCHOOL FOLKS SAY, "BIRDS OF A FEATHER FLOCK TOGETHER", AND THEN THERE'S "YOU ARE WHO YOU HANG OUT WITH". WHO'S YOUR CREW?... THAT WILL GENERALLY DETERMINE WHO YOU ARE OR WHERE YOU'RE GOING.

THE BIBLE SAYS THAT AS A MAN THINKETH IN HIS HEART SO IS HE.

WHATEVER YOU WANT TO BE, START HANGING OUT WITH THOSE WHO ARE THERE. IF YOU WANT TO BE A GOOD LAWYER, HANG OUT WITH GOOD LAWYERS. IF YOU WANT TO BE A GOOD CRIMINAL, HANG OUT WITH GOOD CRIMINALS. ETC. ETC. ETC... WHY? BECAUSE WHATEVER YOU WANT TO BECOME YOU NEED TO SURROUND YOURSELF WITH IT. DOING SO WILL CHANGE YOUR MIND

OR VIEW. EVENTUALLY CHANGING YOUR MIND OR VIEW WILL DROP DOWN INTO YOUR HEART AND WHATEVER IS IN YOUR HEART YOU WILL EVENTUALLY BECOME. WHY? BECAUSE YOUR HEART IS YOUR LIFE. IT'S AT THE CORE OF YOUR VERY BEING. WHATEVER IS IN YOUR HEART WILL DISPLAY ITSELF IN YOUR LIFE. THE HEART IS KIND OF AT THE CORE OF THE SOUL. THE SOUL OF A PERSON IS THEIR MIND, WILL AND EMOTIONS.

KING SOLOMON (GUY FROM BIBLICAL TIMES WHO WAS BASICALLY THE RICHEST AND WISEST GUY EVER TO EXIST) SAID, "GUARD YOUR HEART FOR OUT OF IT FLOWS THE ISSUES OF YOUR LIFE". IT'S VERY IMPORTANT WHO YOU ALLOW IN YOUR INNER CIRCLE. THEY HAVE DIRECT ACCESS TO YOUR HEART. IT'S VITAL WHOM YOU CHOOSE AS A SPOUSE... OR WHOM YOU GET HOOKED UP WITH. THEY. LIKE NO ONE ELSE. HAVE A DIRECT LINE TO YOUR HEART. I'M SURE YOU'VE HEARD THE OLD SAYING "THE RIGHT WOMAN CAN MAKE YOU & THE WRONG ONE CAN BREAK YOU". WHY IS IT THAT YOUR SIBLINGS ARE ABLE TO MAKE YOU FURIOUS LIKE NO OTHER? BECAUSE THEY ARE IN YOUR INNER CIRCLE. THEY HAVE ACCESS TO YOUR HEART. A SIBLING CAN SAY SOMETHING TO YOU AND A GUY OFF OF THE STREET CAN SAY

THE EXACT SAME WORDS WITH THE EXACT SAME INTENT BUT WHEN YOUR SIBLING SAYS IT TO YOU, YOU FLIP DA FCK OUT OR IT HURTS YOU, RUINING YOUR WHOLE WEEK. PROXIMITY. BE CAREFUL WHAT YOU SURROUND YOUR SELF WITH AS THEY WILL DETERMINE YOUR FUTURE OR SERIOUSLY INFLUENCE IT.

YOUR ONLY OLD IF YOU ACCEPT THAT. BEING OLD REALLY JUST SPEAKS TO OR OF A MINDSET. FEAR OFTEN CLOAKS ITSELF IN WISDOM. DO YOU THINK WITH RESERVATIONS THAT YOU ONCE NEVER HAD? WHAT'S AT THE ROOT OF IT? WHY IS IT THERE NOW BUT "I NEVER USED TO BE THAT WAY?". NOT ALL THOUGHT PROCESSES, RESERVATIONS, CHANGES ARE FOR THE BETTER. THEY DEVELOP AS A RESULT OF IN INWARD CHANGE TO YOUR HEART. AN INFRACTION, HURT, MISTRUST, DOUBT, DISCOURAGMENT, INCIDENT, LOW SELF-ESTEEM, ANY CRAP THAT HAPPENED AS A RESULT OF LETTING SOMEONE TO CLOSE TO YOUR INNER CIRCLE RESULTING IN AN OFFENSE OR THEM SPEAKING SOMETHING INTO YOUR LIFE. YOUTH IS A MINDSET. YOUR NEVER TO OLD TO LIVE. LIFE IS SIMPLY MEANT TO BE LIVED. HOWEVER, MOST PEAPLE WON'T TELL YOU THAT. MOST PEAPLE INWARDLY HATE THE FACT IF YOU DO OFTEN, NOT

REALIZING THEY'RE EVEN DOING SO (JEALOUS OF YOU LIVING LIFE). YOU DON'T HAVE TO BE A HATER CREATOR (FLAUNT ACHEIVEMENTS) IN ORDER FOR PEAPLE TO HATE THE WAY YOU LIVE, THE THINGS YOU OWN & THE SUCCESSES YOU HAVE... A LOT OF PEAPLE WILL DO THAT ALL ON THEIR OWN.

NEVER STOP DREAMING, NEVER BE AFRAID, TO DO.

YOU MIGHT NOT MAKE IT, OR PERHAPS ONE DAY YOU TRIED SOMETHING & YOU FAILED OR CAME UP SHORT OF YOUR ORIGINAL PLAN. DREAM AGAIN. KEEP GOING. DON'T LET SOME HARD TIMES GET IN THE WAY OF THE BIG PICTURE OF YOUR LIFE. SOME PEAPLE HAVE STRUGGLE AFTER STRUGGLE... YOU STILL SHOULDN'T QUIT. JUST TAKE IN THE VIEW ONCE IN A WHILE LOOKING AT THE BIG PICTURE.

LIFE IS FULL OF COMINGS AND GOINGS. SOME VENTURE'S LOADED WITH BAGGAGE, SOME WITHOUT. SOME VENTURE'S TAKE YOU TO MOUNTAIN TOPS SOME TO NOTHING SPECIAL. YOUR MINDSET IS THE ONE THING THAT WILL EITHER, BRING LIFE OUT OF YOUR ADVENTURE'S OR MISERY. NEVER FORGET TO KEEP ABREAST OF LIFE AS A WHOLE, IN TERMS OF VIEW. DON'T LET EVERY LITTLE THING GET TO YOU. THERE'S ALWAYS A

LITTLE TURBULANCE IN FLIGHT. SOMETIME'S MORE, SOMETIME'S LESS. YOU CAN'T LET THAT CHANGE THE WHOLE OF YOU OR YOUR FLIGHT. LOOK AT THE BIG PICTURE. EVEN EAGLE'S HIT THERMAL'S. THEY USE THEM TO PROPELL THEM UP AND INTO THE NEXT THING. IT'S IMPORTANT TO TAKE AN EAGLE'S VIEW ON YOUR LIFE AND/OR THE PROBLEMS IN IT FROM TIME TO TIME. LOOKING AT THINGS FROM A MOUNTAIN TOP VIEW FROM TIME TO TIME WILL GIVE YOU A PROPER PERSPECTIVE. A DISSASSOCIATIVE ONE. ONE WHERE, WHEN YOUR VIEW IS SO FAR FROM YOUR SITUATION IT LOSES ITS INFLUENCE OR THREAT ALLOWING YOU TO BREATH AND FOCUS ON WHAT'S IMPORTANT. HAVING A COACH IN YOUR CORNER IS VITAL. SOMETIMES WE DON'T HAVE THAT LUXURY (HAVING A COACH) SO, WE HAVE TO MAN THAT POSITION OURSELVES. TAKE A STEP BACK FROM TIME TO TIME ASSESSING THE SITUATION. IN THE HEAT OF BATTLE YOUR FOCUS IS LIMITED. YOU NEED AN EAGLE'S EYE APPROACH IN ORDER TO SEE THE BIG PICTURE. WHERE HAVE YOU BEEN? WHERE ARE YOU HEADED? WHAT'S COMING AT YOU? WHAT ARE YOU DEALING WITH? WHAT IS THE TERRAIN AHEAD? BEHIND, AND ALL AROUND? BUMPS IN THE ROAD? YOU NEED AN UNBIASED REVIEW. YOU CAN

ONLY GET THAT IF YOU VIEW IT FROM AFAR WHERE THE PRESSURE IS LESS THREATENING. LESS HEATED.

SOMETIME'S YOU MIGHT HAVE TO CALL IT. SOMETIMES YOU MIGHT HAVE TO SELF-ARREST BECAUSE, OF WHERE YOU ARE GOING.

LET THE HATERS HATE, DARE TO DREAM. DARE TO FOLLOW THEM(DREAMS). DON'T LET ANYONE STOP YOU. YOU ONLY REALLY DIE WHEN YOU STOP DREAMING.

RISK

SOMETIMES YOU CAN'T LEAVE ANYTHING FOR THE RETURN TRIP BACK.

THERE ARE THOSE RARE MOMENTS IN LIFE WHEN IN WHICH YOU HAVE TO GO ALL IN.

ALWAY'S CONSIDER THE COST. CAN YOU AFFORD TO LOSE WHATEVER YOU PUT IN THE POT? ARE THE POTENTIAL REPERCUSSIONS WORTH IT? IT'S OK TO WALK AWAY. SOMETIMES THOUGH, YOU NEED CHANGE SO PROFUSELY YOU HAVE TO DRAW THE LINE NEVER GOING BACK. DO IT.

SOMETIMES, THERE'S SIMPLY THIS DESIRE JUST TO PUSH THE BAR, SET THE STANDARD. JUST BECAUSE... DO IT WITHOUT REGRET. WHY? BECAUSE YOU ARE LIVING.

I DON'T THINK I HAVE HEARD OF ONE STORY OF ANYONE WHO WAS "A REAL-WORLD- SHAKER" (HOMAGE TO "COOL HAND LUKE") WHERE THAT

WAS THEIR ONLY GOAL. TO MAKE HISTORY. TO BE KNOWN. TO BE HONEST ANYONE WHO HAS EVER BEEN ANYONE OF ANY NOTE, ONLY DID SO BECAUSE THEY FOLLOWED THE DESIRES IN THEIR HEART NOT LOOKING BACK. TUNNEL VISION. THEY FOLLOWED THE CODE INSCRIBED ON THEIR HEART AND JUST. DID. UNRELENTING, ALL IN, NOT LOOKING BACK, CONSIDERING ALL THAT AT RISK AS LOST IN PURSUIT OF THE END RESULT OR GOAL.

HISTORY WAS MADE BY PEAPLE AND THEIR CODE.

&...THEN THERE ARE ALSO THOSE TIMES YOU HAVE NO CHOICE BUT, TO GO ALL IN. SOMETIMES, THE ONLY DIRECTION YOU HAVE TO GO IS UP. IF THAT'S THE CASE, DO. NOT. LET CIRCUMSTANCES DEFEAT YOU. THERE'S ALWAYS A WAY THROUGH, OVER, AROUND (IN SOME CASES) ... IT MAY NOT BE FUN, IT MAY REALLY SUCK *SS BUT, YOU WILL SURVIVE. JUST FOCUS ON THE NEXT THING AND. KEEP. PRESSING. YOU CAN WIN IF YOU DO NOT QUIT. IT'S IMPOSSIBLE TO NOT PUT FORTH ENERGY WITHOUT OBTAINING SOME KIND OF RESULT.

IT'S A LAW OF THE UNIVERSE. ANY EFFORT PUT FORTH IT WILL COME BACK TO YOU, MAYBE NOT AS YOU PLANNED BUT, IT WILL COME BACK AROUND NONETHELESS.

AUTHORITY

OBEDIENCE = AUTHORITY = SUCCESS

SOME OF YOU MAY WANT TO SKIP OVER THIS CHAPTER AS IT LEANS TO HEAVY TOWARDS NOT BEING YOUR THING. (TOO RELIGIOUS) I'M PERSONALLY BIG ON AUTHORITY. I HATE PEAPLE WHO UNDERMINE THEIR LEADERS. GRATES AT THE VERY FIBER OF MY SOUL. BACK IN THE DAY I WOULDN'T HESITATE TO DROP SOMEONE COMMITTING THIS VERY ACT.

THE BIBLE IS CLEAR ABOUT HOW AUTHORITY IS TO BE VIEWED AND ACKNOWLEDGED. ROMANS 13:1-2 LOOSELY STATES THAT THERE IS NO AUTHORITY EXCEPT THAT WHICH GOD HAS ESTABLISHED, AND HE WHO RESISTS THAT AUTHORITY RESISTS GOD... THE BIBLE IN PROVERBS 21:1 LOOSELY STATES THAT "THE HEART OF THE KING IS IN THE HAND OF THE

LORD AND HE DIRECTS IT AS THE WATERCOURSES IN THIS LIFE..."

YOUR BOSS, AUTHORITY FIGURE, LEADER, MAY BE A TOP KNOTCH PIECE OF CRAP. BUT IF YOU GRASP THIS PRINCIPLE, IT WILL PROPEL YOU TO WHERE YOU NEED TO OR WANT TO BE.

PSALMS 75:6-7 LOOSELY STATES THAT "PROMOTION COMES NEITHER FROM THE EAST OR THE WEST BUT FROM THE HAND OF THE LORD."

PSALMS 91:1-4 LOOSELY STATES THAT "THOSE WHO LIVE IN THE SHADOW OF THE ALMIGHTY WILL FIND REFUGE UNDER HIS WINGS."

PROVERBS 9:10 LOOSELY STATES THAT "THE FEAR (RESPECT FOR) OF THE LORD IS THE BEGINNING OF WISDOM."

JOHN 15:4 LOOSELY STATES THAT "ABIDE IN ME AND I IN YOU AND I WILL GIVE YOU THE DESIRES OF YOUR HEART."

MATHEW 7:9 LOOSELY STATES THAT "WHAT GOOD FATHER IF ASKED BY HIS SON FOR BREAD WILL HE GIVE HIM A STONE?"

PSALM 50:10 LOOSELY STATES THAT "GOD OWNS THE CATTLE ON 1000 HILLS (EVERYTHING IS HIS)."

ALL OF THAT BEING SAID... THE KEY TO SUCCESS IS OBEDIENCE, EITHER TO YOUR

AUTHORITY FIGURE AND/OR GOD DIRECTLY AS IT'S ONE IN THE SAME. BEING OBEDIENT PUTS YOU IN AUTHORITY BECAUSE YOU'RE SIDING WITH THE ONE IN AUTHORITY BY CHOOSING TO YIELD TO HIS WAYS. THE NATURAL OUTCOME OF THAT IS SUCCESS, BLESSING, ABUNDANCE. WHATEVER YOU WANNA LABEL IT.

BY CHOOSING TO YIELD TO (RESPECT) AND HONOR WHOEVER IS IN AUTHORITY OVER YOUR LIFE OR A PART OF YOUR LIFE.... AND I'M NOT SAYING SOMEONE WHO IS OBVIOUSLY OUT OF LINE PUTTING YOU AT RISK OR IN HARMS WAY. (IE. DOMESTIC ABUSE, ABUSE, SOMEONE WHO STEALS FROM YOU, ETC. ETC...) YOU'RE CHOOSING TO KNOWINGLY OR UNKNOWINGLY HONOR GOD. IN DOING SO, YOU'RE CHOOSING TO LET HIM BE RESPONSIBLE FOR YOU (ABIDING IN THE SHADOW...). BY CHOOSING TO LET HIM BE RESPONSIBLE FOR YOU, YOUR "ABIDING IN THE VINE" AS THEY SAY... OR "ABIDING IN HIM (HIS WAYS/METHODS)." IN "ABIDING IN HIM/HIS WAYS/ METHODS ETC." YOU'RE LETTING YOURSELF BE IN CLOSE PROXIMITY WITH HIM (AS YOU'RE FOLLOWING HIS WILL/HEART). IN DOING SO, YOU POSITION YOURSELF FOR BLESSING. OR HIS HAND. BY DEFAULT, FOR BEING OBEDIENT, YOU

BECOME CLOSE TO HIM OR HIS WAYS... HIS FACE, OR RATHER WHO HE IS. IN SEEKING HIS FACE (CHOOSING TO FOLLOW HIS METHODS) YOU, GET HIS HAND(BLESSING), SOMETHING THAT GIVES...

IF YOUR CLOSE TO SOMEONE AND THEY SINCERELY CARE THEY WILL GIVE YOU ANYTHING PROVIDED THEY COULD. GOD IS THE PERFECT MANAGER. HE IS ALSO A GOD OF MULTIPLICATION. EVERYTHING HE DOES HAS MULTIPLE FACETS TO IT AND HE WILL GET SOMETHING POSITIVE FROM ALL OF IT. GOD CAN TWEAK A CIRCUMSTANCE, CUSTOM TAILORED TO YOUR SITUATION JUST TO BENEFIT, BLESS, OR PROMOTE YOU IN SPITE OF YOUR CIRCUMSTANCES. SOMETIMES ALL YOU HAVE TO DO IS ASK. GOD HAS NO PROBLEM PUTTING YOU IN CHARGE OF OR SPEARHEADING SOMETHING YOU CREATE. HE JUST WANTS TO BE A PART OF IT.

DON'T JUST SEEK THE HAND. SEEK THE FACE. THE HAND(PROVISION)WILL COME WITH.

FEAR

EMOTION IS NOT AUTHORITY. IN ORDER TO BE IN AUTHORITY OVER A SITUATION YOU FIRST HAVE TO NOT BE MOVED BY IT. MOST PEOPLE'S KNEE JERK SOLUTION TO A PERCIEVED THREAT IS REACTION. IF YOU'VE EVER PLAYED THE FLINCH GAME AS A KID YOU'LL RELATE. IN ORDER TO PLAY THE GAME, YOU WALK UP TO SOMEONE AND ACT AS THOUGH YOUR ABOUT TO PUNCH THEM IN THE FACE OR SOMEWHERE, COMING AS CLOSE AS YOU CAN IN ORDER TO GET THEM TO FLINCH... OR REACT IN SOME MANNER. IF THEY FLINCH YOU THEN GET TO HIT THEM IN THE SHOULDER OR SOMETHING AND SAY (IN THE VOICE OF NELSON FROM THE SIMPSON'S) YOU FLINCHED! HAHA!) SO, IN ORDER TO CONTROL SOMEONE ALL ONE WOULD HAVE TO DO IS MAKE THEM REACT. MOST PEAPLE HAVE PATTERNS AND RESPOND THE SAME

WAY EVERYTIME. ALL I NEED TO DO IS FIGURE OUT WHAT YOUR TYPICAL RESPONSE WOULD BE AND THEN I COULD CONTROL YOU SIMPLY BY PERVOKING A REACTION FROM YOU.

THE UMBRELLA OF FEAR HAS TWO SUB-UMBRELLA'S OR RESPONSES. FIGHT OR FLIGHT. THE FIGHT OR FLIGHT UMBRELLA'S HAVE MANY SUB-UMBRELLA'S UNDER THEM, AND UNDER THOSE UMBRELLA'S YEP, MORE UMBRELLA'S. NOW, THAT YOU HAVE A PICTURE IN YOUR HEAD OF THIS MULTI-TIERED TREE OF UMBRELLA'S... TURN THE TREE UPSIDE DOWN PUTTING FEAR AT THE BOTTOM OR AT THE ROOT OF IT.

I THINK JOYCE MEYER IS THE ORIGINATOR OF THIS ACRONYM. IF NOT, THAT'S WHERE I HEARD IT FROM ANYWAY, AND IT'S ROCKIN.

FEAR. FALSE, EVIDENCE, APPEARING, REAL... MOST FEARS ARE SIMPLY MISPERCEPTIONS. FALSE TRUTHS BASED ON OUR HISTORY, & IMAGINATIONS.

THINKING ABOUT WHAT YOU ARE THINKING ABOUT. IS IT ROOTED IN INSECURITIES, STRESS, MISTRUST, PHOBIAS, ANXIETIES, DISALLUSIONS, APPREHENSION? WHY? IT ALL STARTED SOMEWHERE. FEAR IS LEARNED. THAT'S WHY CHILDREN ARE FEARLESS. THEY HAVEN'T HAD ENOUGH TIME TO DEVELOP ANY. FEAR WILL

CAUSE YOU TO DO A NUMBER OF THINGS IF YOU LET IT.

AS A BOY, AND TO THIS DAY I HATE WEREWOLVES AND WEREWOLF MOVIES. THE MOVIE SILVER BULLET FREAKED ME OUT AS A KID. EVEN NOW I HATE HORROR MOVIES ALL TOGETHER. I DON'T WATCH THEM. I HATE THAT FEELING OF FEAR YOU GET. I TRY TO KEEP THAT TO A MINIMUM TOO... IF I DO HAPPEN TO WATCH A HORROR MOVIE, I HAVE TO WATCH 2 "GOOD" MOVIES AFTER JUST TO CLEANSE MY HEAD. LOL HOW MANY OF YOU HAVE WATCHED A SCARY MOVIE ONLY TO AFTER DOING SO, WALK THROUGH THE HOUSE OR SOMEWHERE AND HEARING A NOISE CAUSES YOU TO TENSE UP AND FREEZE, OR GRAB WHATEVER IS AROUND READY TO CRACK SOMEONES SKULL?... WHEN AT THE END OF IT, NONE OF IT IS REAL. WEREWOLVES AREN'T REAL. NOT THE KIND PORTRAYED IN MOVIES ANYWAY. BUT I STILL HAVE A RESPONSE AT TIMES, BASED ON THE IMAGES THAT I REACT TO, AFTER LETTING THEM PLAY THROUGH MY BRAIN. LOL THERE IS A PSYCHOLOGICAL TERM CALLED THE PAVLOVIAN RESPONSE. IT'S BASICALLY A CONDITIONED RESPONSE. YOU CAN LET YOURSELVE BE CONDITIONED TOWARDS MINDSETS ROOTED

IN FEAR. I THINK EVERYONE HAS... IT'S HUMAN NATURE. IF YOU CAN ALLOW YOURSELF TO BE CONDITIONED TOWARDS FEAR YOU CAN ALLOW YOURSELF TO BE CONDITIONED WITHOUT. OUR BRAIN IS A TOOL, A MUSCLE, IF YOU WILL. MAKE IT WORK FOR YOU. BE IN CONTROL OF IT FOR A CHANGE. WHOEVER TOLD US THAT IT(BRAIN) HAS TO CONTROL US? WHEN IS IT EXACTLY, THAT WE AS HUMANS BOUGHT INTO THAT IDEA ANYWAY (THAT WE'RE SUBJECT TO OUR BRAIN)? IT'S OK TO FEEL FEAR. THAT'S WHAT KEEPS YOU ALIVE. JUST DON'T LET IT CONTROL YOU.

BE THANKFUL

BEING THANKFUL, GRATEFUL, AND SHOWING OR
EXTENDING GRATITUDE TO ANYONE WHO HAS
HELPED YOU ALONG THE WAY DENY IT OR NOT,
IS SIMPLY A PART OF THE NATURAL PROCESS
OF LIFE IF YOU WILL. IT'S AS THOUGH YOU TAP
INTO THIS HIDDEN CISTERN THAT OPENS DOORS
TO THIS OTHERWISE CLOSED REALM SIMPLY
BY HAVING AN ATTITUDE OF BEING THANKFUL.
SOMETIMES YOU SIMPLY HAVE NO CHOICE IN THE
MATTER. SOMETIMES THE SAFEST PLACE IS IN THE
EYE OF THE STORM. THAT CAN BE A HUMBLING
EXPERIENCE. YOU HAVE NO CHOICE BUT TO
RECEIVE HELP. I FIRMLY BELIEVE WHAT GOES
AROUND COMES AROUND. HELPING PEAPLE AND
BEING THANKFUL FOR BEING HELPED IS PART OF
THE BALANCE OF LIFE. EVERYONE IS AFRAID TO BE
THANKFUL ANYMORE. THIS WHOLE CULTURE OF "I

CAN AND WILL DO IT ALONE" IS A MISNOMER BASED MORE IN PRIDE THAN AS OPPOSED TO ANYTHING ELSE. I WAS ALWAYS THIS GUY THAT WOULD NEVER RECEIVE ANYTHING FROM ANYONE EVEN IF IT HURT ME BAD. I HAD MY LOGICAL REASONING FOR ALL OF IT FOR SURE..."ONE DAY THAT FAVOR WILL BE USED AGAINST YOU... (MANIPULATION), OR ONE DAY YOU'LL HEAR ABOUT IT AGAIN FOR SURE". NOT THAT THAT ALL DOESN'T HAVE ITS PLACE (NOT AT ALL SAYING IT'S OK TO MANIPULATE SOMETIMES). BUT I WAS SIMPLY CONVINCED THAT I WAS STRONGER BY NOT RECEIVING HELP EVEN IF IT WAS PAINFUL AND PUT ME IN A REALLY BAD SPOT AT THE TIME. TRUTH BE TOLD, IF "WHAT GOES AROUND COMES AROUND", "YOU REAP WHAT YOU SEW", "KARMA", OR WHATEVER, YOU STEAL SOMEONE'S BLESSING BY NOT ALLOWING THEM TO HELP YOU. WHY? BECUASE, YOU DON'T ALLOW THEM TO SEW A POSITIVE SEED, OR YOU DON'T ALLOW THEM TO START "PAYING IT FORWARD".

THERE IS A BALANCE TO EVERYTHING FOR SURE... YOU OBVIOUSLY WANT TO HAVE SOME SORT OF GRIT IN YOUR CHARACTER AND BEING WILLING TO GO TOE TO TOE WITH THE TASK(S) SET BEFORE YOU NOT BEING SO LAZY THAT ALL YOU DO IS RELY ON EVERYONE ELSE... BUT AT THE END

OF THE DAY IT'S OK TO RECEIVE. LET PEAPLE HELP
YOU. LISTEN TO SOMEONE ONCE IN A WHILE.

IT'S OK TO BE YOU.

MAKE YOUR LIFE STAMPED WITH:

"DOES NOT APPLY".

ACKNOWLEDGEMENTS

I WOULD LIKE TO TAKE THE TIME TO THANK EVERYONE WHO BOTH KNOWINGLY AND UNKNOWINGLY HELPED MAKE THIS POSSIBLE... NOT IN ANY PRIME ORDER... ONLY THOSE I COULD SCRATCH DOWN FAST, AS I DID THIS BOOK IN A DAY. THERE ARE TOO MANY PEOPLE I FORGOT.

MY WIFE AND MY KIDS... FOR BEING AN ENDLESS POSITIVE MOTIVATION AND FOR HELPING ME TAKE THE TIME TO STEP BACK, RELAX, AND ENJOY LIFE.

MY AUNT AND UNCLE FOR PUTTING ME UP, GIVING ME THE TIME I NEEDED TO RELAX AND FINISH THIS BOOK. I MISS THE SMELL OF BUTTERED GRITS, BISCUITS, BACON, & EGGS COOKING AND COFFEE BREWING EVERY SUNDAY LIKE CLOCKWORK AND ALWAYS LEAVING A LIGHT ON IN MY ROOM FOR ME TO COME HOME TO WHEN I WAS GONE.

CONTACT INFO:

JASON T ROGERS

EMAIL:
JASONTROGERS9@GMAIL.COM

JASON T ROGERS
P.O. BOX 645
BELOIT, WI.
53512 U.S.A.